T0316703

THE GLOBAL MANAGEMENT SERIES

Commercial Law in a Global Context

Yvonne McLaren and Josephine Bisacre

 Goodfellow Publishers Ltd

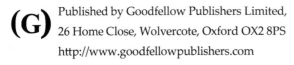

Published by Goodfellow Publishers Limited,
26 Home Close, Wolvercote, Oxford OX2 8PS
http://www.goodfellowpublishers.com

British Library Cataloguing in Publication Data: a catalogue record for this
title is available from the British Library.
Library of Congress Catalog Card Number: on file.

ISBN: 978-1-911396-12-3

 Design and typesetting by P.K. McBride, www.macbride.org.uk

Cover design by Cylinder

Printed by Baker & Taylor, www.baker-taylor.com

Contents

To my partner Duncan for his continued love and support and my students past, present and future who make the darker days brighter.

YMcL

To the other authors of this book who have brought an international outlook to the study of Scots law in their writing, and to my long-suffering husband Jim for his listening skills.

JB

Biographies

The editors

Josephine Bisacre is an Associate Professor of Business Law at Heriot-Watt University and is the Director of Undergraduate Studies in the School of Management & Languages at Heriot-Watt University. She formerly worked as a lecturer and senior lecturer at Edinburgh Napier University and as a solicitor in private practice in the field of corporate law. She is the author of various book chapters in the area of business law, which include a chapter on sources of law in Black, G (ed) (2015) *Business Law in Scotland* 3rd edition. Edinburgh: W. Green, a chapter on the European Citizen and Consumer in the second edition of Johnston, D and Turner, C (2015) *European Business*, 3rd edition, Routledge, and wrote two chapters for the second edition of McManus, F and Russell, E., (2011) *Delict: a Comprehensive Guide to the Law of Scotland*, Dundee: Dundee University Press, as well as various contributions on company law. She has experience of teaching and examining on business law courses offered by various professional bodies.

Yvonne McLaren is an Aberdeen University Law School Graduate currently based within the School of Management and Languages at Heriot-Watt University. In addition to the role as director in Safeguard Technical Services Ltd, Yvonne has a variety of roles within the department, including course leader in the Law of International Human Resource Management, Commercial Law, and Marketing and Consumer Law. Pastoral duties include being the Third year co-ordinator and engaging with students in the role of first year super-mentor. Yvonne has previously taught a variety of law subjects at the University of the West of Scotland and Glasgow College of Commerce.

Contributors

Zeenat Beebeejaun is the founder of Pearl Legal, a legal consultancy firm established in the United Arab Emirates specializing in Commercial Law. She is also a lecturer in law at Heriot Watt University in Dubai. Prior to her law career, Zeenat studied Pharmacy in the UK where she also practiced for a few years. Her varied educational background has enabled her to relate to different working professionals and she is often invited to talk in panel discussions focusing on legal issues encountered by UAE start ups. In addition, Zeenat has also appeared as a guest writer in a leading women's magazine in the Gulf region.

Bahma Sivasubramaniam is a barrister of the Honourable Society of Lincoln's Inn and was admitted to the Malaysian bar in 1987 as an Advocate and Solicitor. She was in practice for twelve years during which she served as a member of the Kuala Lumpur Bar Committee for three consecutive terms. Her practice was mainly on banking and commercial matters and she did criminal practice on a pro bono basis. She was also a member of the Human Rights, Charity & Welfare and Publications Committees of the Bar Council. She left the bar to do a Ph.D. at the University of Durham under the Chevening Scholarship of the British Council. She then decided to pursue an academic career, and has been teaching at Multimedia University, top private university in Malaysia, for the past ten years. She teaches various subjects including Employment law and industrial relations, Business law, Law for Engineers, and Cyberlaw. When she was in practice, Bahma campaigned for the right for women barristers to wear trousers to court – and succeeded!

Jill Stirling is an Assistant Professor of Business and Consumer Law, in the School of Management and Languages at Heriot-Watt University. With a degree in History, Politics and Philosophy from Edinburgh University, and a postgraduate diploma in Financial Studies from Heriot-Watt, Jill finally decided on law as a career and is admitted to practice as a solicitor in Scotland and Hong Kong. She has worked in private practice in Scotland and Hong Kong, as a government lawyer in Scotland, and in the corporate sector in Hong Kong. She was a Lecturer in Law at the University of Hong Kong for thirteen years, during which time she was also a member of the Hong Kong Inland Revenue Board of Review, hearing tax appeals, and chaired the Hong Kong University Academic Staff Association. Her current interests are all aspects of consumer law, and tax, with particular emphasis on the need for governments to deal with the aggressive tax planning of multi-national companies.

Preface

This book was conceived as part of a series of business management textbooks that would be used when teaching students on international business management programmes, where students might be studying the same programme but in several different locations: some might be in Scotland, while others might be in various other countries dotted around the globe. The important thing was that the course must be equally relevant for everyone regardless of location.

Colleagues writing in most areas of the syllabus of a business management degree should be able to meet this challenge by making sure that appropriate examples from across the globe are used. But for those engaged in globalised legal education the challenge is greater, particularly if the legal system in question is a small one such as Scots law. Students from elsewhere in the world might be studying the subject in Scotland, while students who are taking a degree offered by a Scottish university may study the subject in some distant country. This means that the subject must be taught in a way that is mindful of the fact that there are other families of legal systems that operate in different ways, and while some solutions may be similar between the laws of different countries, others will be different. The topic must be relevant for everyone to study. Fortunately in commercial law, unlike other areas of law, there is much common ground between English law and Scots law.

The core of the book is that of a textbook on certain elements of commercial law namely the law of contract, the law of delict, and the law of agency, and it can be used simply as such. However, the book also attempts to set Scots law in its global context by exploring the place of Scots law in the families of legal systems, and it includes two chapters that focus on the legal systems of the United Arab Emirates and Malaysia, which are examples of the two main legal traditions: civil law and common law. Because for many students this will be the only legal course they will do, the book includes some information in Chapter 1 on how to study law.

The writing team is similarly global: three of us are based in Scotland, and the other two work in Dubai and Malaysia respectively. One of our number has extensive experience lecturing in higher education in Hong Kong. It would be nice some time to be able to meet as a writing team in one place, but instead our discussions generally take place over weak connections on Skype, WhatsApp, and endless emails.

We hope that the result is a book that will provide straightforward explanations of concepts, avoiding jargon, in order to aid student learning. In our view the chapters on the two other legal systems will prove interesting to those who are not based in those countries, as well as to those who are.

Yvonne McLaren and Josephine Bisacre

1 Scots Commercial Law in a Global Context

Josephine Bisacre

People study commercial law at college or university for all kinds of reasons. It may be as part of a law degree, where a detailed knowledge of the subject will be called for and other legal subjects will be studied. Equally the subject may be studied as part of an accountancy or business management degree or college course. Students from other subject areas may decide to study it as an elective, realising that a basic level of knowledge of the subject would be useful to a person with a career in engineering, computing, business or the creative arts. Increasingly, students are electing to study all or part of their programmes abroad, and universities offer their programmes at various overseas campuses, or by distance learning, with the result that students might find themselves studying Scots law at a campus in places far from Scotland such as Bangladesh or Mauritius, or an international student might be studying at a university or college in Scotland. This chapter seeks to explain the relevance of Scots law to students whose main specialism is not law, and to those who live, work and study thousands of miles away from Scotland, or who come from another country and spend a short time studying in Scotland. It also gives practical advice on how to study and write about commercial law. Equally, this book is suitable as a course text for those who are from Scotland and studying the subject in Scotland.

How does Scots Law fit into the global family of legal systems?

Legal systems are products of their history. Until 1707 Scotland and England were separate countries and had separate legal systems, and spent many centuries fighting each other. From 1603 they had the same king but separate parliaments and governments before fully uniting in 1707. After the Acts of Union of 1706-7, some aspects of the legal system of Scotland continued to be distinct: Scotland retained separate courts and much of its own substantive law, though all legislation thereafter came from the parliament in Westminster, London. Because England and Scotland had such a turbulent past and the two countries were often at war in the years before the union of the parliaments, Scots lawyers preferred to take ideas from Roman law and continental legal systems such as the Netherlands, France and Italy, rather than from English law. These legal systems were based on Roman law. After the union of the parliaments, the main influence started to come from England, and Scots law is said to be a mixed legal system, drawing on both the common law tradition (England) and the civil law tradition (continental legal systems).

Later, after the union of the parliaments, English influence became more pronounced. These influences were very different, as two different legal traditions were in play. Other legal systems have grown up in other parts of the world as a result of the development of various political and religious systems. Examples are socialist legal systems and Islamic legal systems but there are many others.

During the late twentieth century, as Scotland came to have a rather different political outlook from England, demand arose for devolution of law-making powers to Scotland, and since 1999 there has been a Scottish parliament and Scottish government at Holyrood in Edinburgh with devolved powers in certain areas of law. Over time the devolved powers have expanded, and Scotland now has some tax-raising powers. It is likely that this move towards further devolution of powers will continue in future. There was a referendum in Scotland in 2014 on possible independence from the rest of the United Kingdom, but the vote was to remain as part of the UK.

The common law family

English law was the first member of this family. Historically, the principal source of law in these legal systems was the courts, which decided and developed the law through its application in cases. This approach is quite pragmatic. English law was applied throughout its colonies in the colonial era. Members of this family include Scotland (though as stated, Scots law is a mixed system), the USA, Canada, and many commonwealth countries such as Nigeria. In the common law legal tradition, the law advances incrementally from case to case, as precedents are applied to later cases, which enables it to develop as society's needs change. The legal system of Malaysia, which is discussed in Chapter 4, is a member of this family, as a consequence of being a former British colony.

The Romano-Germanic family (civil law)

These legal systems had their origin in the *ius civile* of Roman law. In this legal tradition principles of the law are codified, starting from the later period of the Roman Empire, and there is a close link in this family between law and ethics. Principles from the codes are then applied in cases. Countries whose legal systems are part of this legal tradition include France, Germany, Italy and the Netherlands, and civil law was also exported to Louisiana in the USA, to Japan and to Egypt. Former French colonies such as Algeria are part of this tradition. In this legal tradition, there is less emphasis on judicial precedent than in the common law tradition. The legal system of the United Arab Emirates, discussed in Chapter 3, belongs to this family of legal systems, though Shari'a law is also applied there.

Interestingly, these two families of legal systems have had to work with each other in the European Union, where European law needs to apply to countries from both legal traditions, which often necessitates a great deal of compromise.

Socialist legal systems

Many of the countries that adopted communism were previously members of the Romano-Germanic civil law tradition. When countries adopted communism, it usually happened by revolution, as in Russia, whereupon former laws were repealed and new socialist laws enacted. In some communist states, private law, particularly law on private property, was very limited. China, which is a communist country, is now considered to have a mixed legal system between civil law and customary law. When the former German Democratic Republic, which had been a communist state till 1990, was reunited with West Germany, the socialist laws were repealed and replaced by the laws that operated in West Germany.

■ Islamic legal systems

In Islamic countries, respect for religious laws is generally higher than in western countries, and Islamic law (Shari'a law) is regarded by many in these societies as more important as a guide to conduct than state law. The Koran is the primary source of Islamic law. Islamic law is regarded as immutable because it is religious law, and not adaptable to changing with the needs of society. Chapter 3 will focus on the legal system of the United Arab Emirates and will examine some of these issues further.

Why study Scots commercial law?

The law is one of the elements of the external business environment that every business has to work within. Readers of this book are probably familiar with **PESTEL** analysis, which studies the macro-environmental factors that impact on business, including the legal framework – Political, Economic, Social, Technological, Legal, and Environmental factors. Those who run businesses may not like the law, but they need to know what it is in order to comply with it, otherwise there can be undesirable consequences, such as fines for breaches of criminal law and damages claims where harm results to the public. For those who aspire to become company directors, knowledge of the law is very important, as they and their companies may face potential liabilities under criminal law and civil law if they are do not pay attention to their company's legal position. For example, a decision to reduce the level of maintenance of factory machinery in order to save money, might result in prosecution under health and safety law if people are injured as a result of faults developing in the machinery, and there may also be civil liability to employees and others who are injured.

Commercial law (which may be called by similar names such as business law) is on the curriculum of most universities and colleges where law or accountancy are studied. The accountancy professional bodies call for the study of a syllabus that broadly reflects the contents of this book, plus the law of partnership, company law, the law of trusts, and often aspects of employment law. These syllabuses differ a bit from each other, but they are designed to cover the most important aspects of the subject, and generally focus on the practical aspects of the subject rather than theoretical concepts.

It is important to emphasise that the law is dynamic, and changing all the time as society changes and new issues arise that demand new forms of regulation. For example, as discussed briefly in Chapter 10, the law of defamation in Scotland (in England called 'libel' and 'slander') is outdated and struggling to keep pace with the explosion of information on the internet, the use of Twitter and the like: consequently a proposal for law reform in Scotland has been announced in 2016.

It may seem bizarre to study Scots law outside Scotland, but it is becoming much more common nowadays to study the law of a legal system other than one's own. Students may go on an exchange programme with a university overseas and choose to take legal courses there; they may be studying at a multi-campus university, where a law course is a mandatory part of a programme in which law is just one element, and the same law course is delivered at several international campuses. In these cases, the subject should be studied in context, and where possible, parallels and contrasts with the local legal system should be stressed. The needs of business everywhere in the world are fairly similar, as the problems that arise will be similar: business needs the legal system to be stable, and for the law to be clear. Consequently there are likely to be similarities in the legal solutions that different countries across the world adopt to deal with issues in commercial law, such as breach of contract. There are some general principles of commercial law that are widely applied: while the detail of one particular bit of law might differ from country to country, often at the level of general principles, the law is similar. Time spent studying Scots law is not wasted, even where there is no intention to work in Scotland: an introductory study of Scots commercial law should therefore be transferable, and facilitate the subsequent study of another legal system.

The influences on Scots law

■   Scots law and English law

Chapter 2 of this book gives some of the history of Scots law, a mixed legal system which has taken ideas from both civil law (continental European legal systems) and from common law (English law). It explains the devolved legal system that we have in Scotland: some areas of law are reserved to be legislated on by the UK parliament in London, while others are devolved to the Scottish parliament in Edinburgh.

Scotland is a small country of 5.37 m inhabitants, (Office of National Statistics, 2016). As Scotland has a small population compared with its larger neighbour, England, with a population of 54.78 m (Office of National Statistics, 2016), fewer cases are brought to court in Scotland. This means that there is often no Scottish case on a particular legal point, but there may be a relevant legal case in England on a point of law that is the same in the two countries. This explains why many English cases are referred to in this book.

Scots and English commercial law do differ in some important respects. Probably the most important one is in the law of contract, discussed in Chapters 5 , 6 and 7 of this book. English contract law includes the doctrine of consideration, under which payment of consideration (price of some kind, though it need not be market price) is an essential feature of a valid contract: this is not the case in Scotland. In order not to confuse students, the book does not generally point out these differences.

However, as you might expect, considering the large volume of business conducted by businesses across the UK, many areas of commercial law are identical or nearly so between England, Wales, Scotland, and Northern Ireland. Examples are employment law, the law of partnership, and the law of agency (Chapters 11 and 12 of this book). The law of contract and the law of delict (tort in England) are broadly very similar between Scotland and England, though there are some important differences in the law in these two jurisdictions.

■   The impact of the European Union

The UK joined the EEC (now the European Union, abbreviated here as EU) in 1973. There are 28 member states in the EU, each with their own legal systems. Some are based on civil law, where much of the law is found in codes, while the UK and the Republic of Ireland represent the common law tradition. There are eastern European member states of the EU, such as Poland, that have made the transition from the communist legal tradition. In order to achieve the single market in the EU, some areas of law have been 'harmonised', so that they are made more similar and in some areas identical across the EU, in order to prevent a 'race to the bottom' where business might seek to locate its operations in the member state with the most lax regulations, and in order to promote contracting across borders within the EU. Some areas are the subject of regulations, in order to ensure that the law is identical throughout the member states. For example, following the financial crisis in Europe, the capital adequacy of banks is now the subject of a combination of a regulation and a directive from 2013.

Example: areas of EU law that impact on business

- Rules against discrimination at work
- Rules restricting working time
- Aspects of consumer law including electronic contracting and unfair terms
- Aspects of environmental law, such as restrictions on greenhouse gas emissions by business
- Rules on data protection to protect our privacy
- Rules on commercial agents
- Aspects of company law relating to larger companies, particularly capital and accounting requirements

---

So, some areas of law that affect business may be relatively similar from member state to member state, while others will not. The UK electorate voted in a referendum in June 2016 to exit the EU. That exit will be a big undertaking, entailing much rewriting of law.

International treaties on commercial law

Efforts have been made to make multilateral international treaties on aspects of commercial law, to facilitate global trade. In an ideal world, international contracts between businesses in different countries would be made using one agreed set of rules that are known to those businesses and their advisers. Both parties would then feel comfortable transacting under those rules. Sadly, there are relatively few such international treaties on commercial law, as it is difficult to get a critical number of countries coming from different legal traditions to compromise on the wording of the treaties: every country would like to keep their own legal concepts and rules. After all, their businesses, their lawyers and their courts are used to them. However, there are some treaties that are an exception to this, and have been signed and ratified by a large enough group of countries from across the globe, to have proved very useful.

One of them is the **Vienna Convention on Contracts for the International Sale of Goods** 1980, which was created by UNCITRAL, the United Nations Commission on International Trade Law. Currently 84 states are parties to this convention, the latest signatory being Viet Nam in 2015. The USA, China, and Russia are among the parties to this treaty. Curiously, despite the fact that the UK took part in the drafting on the convention, it has not yet ratified it, perhaps out of a preference for its own laws to be the substantive law applying to a contract. UNCITRAL have produced another convention on the use of electronic communications in international contracts in 2005, which came into force in 2013, but only 7 states have so far adopted it, none of them being large international trading countries.

However, the most useful international treaty of all is UNCITRAL's **Convention on the Recognition and Enforcement of Foreign Arbitral Awards** 1958 (the New York Convention). Many international commercial contracts are decided by arbitration rather than the courts, as there may be technical rather than legal issues involved. Often the decision of the arbitrators has to be enforced on parties in a different country to where the arbitration took place, perhaps because there are assets there. This treaty provides a means of doing this, using the courts of that country, and in the countries to which the convention applies, it is actually easier to enforce an arbitral award than enforce a court judgment, thanks to this treaty. 156 countries – more than half of the countries of the world – have ratified this treaty, and these include the UK, USA, China, Russia, the United Arab Emirates, just to give a few examples.

Exercise

Look up the New York Convention using this link, and check whether your country or the country where you are studying or working, has ratified this convention.

www.uncitral.org/uncitral/en/uncitral_texts/arbitration/NYConvention_status.html

Parties to a contract for the international sale of goods or services should specify in their contract which country's substantive law will apply to the contract and also which country's courts will have jurisdiction in case of a dispute. Often the party with the most bargaining power will succeed in making their legal system the applicable law of the transaction and will also give their courts jurisdiction to hear disputes. This puts the other party at a disadvantage. Where the parties do not specify their own rules in their contract, there is a mechanism for determining this for EU member states, which is found in two EU Regulations. These are beyond the scope of this book.

General principles of commercial law

As has been stated earlier, businesses are essentially outward-looking, always looking for new opportunities, many being exporters and importers of goods. Trade has crossed borders right from ancient times. Merchants from different countries have a very long tradition of meeting each other at trade fairs, where there would often be a system for settling disputes. Some commercial law rules were developed from usages of merchants and became law through general acceptance. It is therefore to be expected that there will be broad similarity between different countries' commercial laws, though the details may differ.

Some countries have a **principle of good faith** as a fundamental part of their law of contract. This is true of France, Germany, the USA, Australia and many others. It is present in most legal systems that are based on the civil law tradition (see Chapter 2).

Example

Article 1 – 304 of the Uniform Commercial Code of the USA

Every contract or duty within the Uniform Commercial Code imposes an obligation of good faith in its performance and enforcement.

In the UK, this obligation of good faith is not universal, though it can be seen in some parts of commercial law. Normally in the UK there is no duty on parties to make positive declarations about matters relating to a contract, unless the terms of the contract call for this, though deliberate deception would be treated differently. Parties in some legal relationships in the UK do have duties that involve good faith, such as employers and employees towards each other; agents and principals owe fiduciary duties as do partners to each other, and the partnership and company directors to their companies. There are some pieces of legislation that originated in the European Union in which the principle of good faith is expressed, and are part of UK law.

Example

S.62 of the Consumer Rights Act 2015

(1) An unfair term of a consumer contract is not binding on the consumer.

(2) An unfair consumer notice is not binding on the consumer.

(3) This does not prevent the consumer from relying on the term or notice if the consumer chooses to do so.

(4) A term is unfair *if, contrary to the requirement of good faith*, it causes a significant imbalance in the parties' rights and obligations under the contract to the detriment of the consumer.

(5) Whether a term is fair is to be determined—

(a) taking into account the nature of the subject matter of the contract,

(b) by reference to all the circumstances existing when the term was agreed and to all of the other terms of the contract or of any other contract on which it depends.

(6) A notice is unfair if, *contrary to the requirement of good faith*, it causes a significant imbalance in the parties' rights and obligations to the detriment of the consumer.

(7) Whether a notice is fair is to be determined—

(a) taking into account the nature of the subject matter of the notice, and

(b) by reference to all the circumstances existing when the rights or obligations to which it relates arose and to the terms of any contract on which it depends....

S.62 of the Consumer Rights Act 2015 represents the enactment of an EU directive. See subsections (4) and (6) where the reference to good faith have been italicised.

The area where the principle of good faith is at its strongest is in insurance law, where the obligations of insured parties towards insurers are *uberrimae fidei,* or 'of the utmost good faith': that obligation demands positive disclosure of matters that might affect the risk, for example that a motorist has been convicted of a driving offence.

The Vienna Convention on international contracts for the sale of goods referred to earlier in this chapter states in Article 7 that in the interpretation of this Convention, "regard is to be had to its international character and to the need to promote uniformity in its application and the observance of good faith in international trade".

When the courts and arbitrators consider cases based on this convention, as with other international conventions, **uniformity** is important: courts should try to adopt a consistent interpretation of the convention, so as to avoid applying rules of domestic law which will vary from country to country. It is important that the cases which are decided under the convention are treated alike, whether they are decided in a court in Dubai or Beijing. UNCITRAL maintains a database of case law so that those who have to decide cases governed by the convention can access at least some of the previous case law.

The main areas of commercial law covered in the book

The book is designed to support university and college courses in commercial law, particularly when the subject is studied in an international context. Courses in commercial law differ in length and in the choice and scope of what is included. As stated earlier, often the choice is influenced by the fact that courses may be accredited by professional bodies which give exemption from their examinations. The book covers the following:

☐ **Scottish legal system** (and two other legal systems) – Chapters 2, 3 and 4 provide a brief introduction to the Scottish legal system and how it relates to the rest of the UK and set it in a global context.

☐ **The law of contract** – Chapters 5, 6 and 7 discuss the law of contract, by which people, including businesses, make voluntary agreements with each other, such as to sell goods and supply services. Breach of contract gives rise to a remedy, generally a claim of damages.

☐ **The law of delict** – Chapters 8, 9, and 10 discuss the law of delict (torts in England), a branch of law which deals with involuntary obligations not to harm others either intentionally or through negligence. As with the law of contract, breach of the law of delict gives rise to a remedy, generally a claim of damages, though the remedies in contract and delict are not identical.

☐ **Agency law** – Chapters 11 and 12, the final chapters in the book, are concerned with the law of agency. Business contracts, particularly international contracts, are often brought about by agents acting for party A, to bring about a contract between party A (the principal) and party B. Again, remedies come into play where the parties have breached their obligations.

How to study commercial law

The study of law is in many ways similar to the study of any other subject at university or college, in that you have first to acquire some knowledge about the subject matter, which will give you an overview of the subject, and also allow you to have some deeper insights into some aspects of the subject matter, and to explore some of the areas where change may be needed. Some students will go on to take further courses in law.

As with the study of any subject, evidence for all your assertions is needed. You cannot just voice an opinion that 'this is not fair' with nothing to back it up. However, in law, in addition to making reference to up-to-date books, articles, and web-based material, you also need to give **legal authority for all your assertions.** This will usually come from a statute or a case (see Chapter 2).

■   Referring to case law

For example, if you are discussing whether a manufacturer of a faulty product has a duty of care to the end-user at common law, you would need to refer to the leading case of *Donoghue v Stevenson* 1932 S.C. (H.L.) 31 (the snail in the ginger beer bottle case, discussed in Chapter 8). Here, not only the name of the case but the **citation** has been given. This is to allow the reader to look it up in the law report where it is published. The case citation includes the year of the case (1932); an abbreviation of the name of the law report (Session Cases, which is the most authoritative series of law reports in Scotland); in this case, an abbreviation of the name of the court where the decision was made (H.L. stands for House of Lords, which was the highest-ranking appeal court and heard appeals in civil matters from the Scottish courts – now replaced by the Supreme Court); and the page reference. If you were referring to this case in an unseen examination, generally examiners are relaxed if you do not give the citation, but the name of the case is important.

Note that the different series of law reports use different conventions in their citations. For example, some use square brackets round the year of the case, some use round brackets and some use no brackets at all. Unless you are going to take your legal studies more seriously and need to understand these conventions, the easiest thing to do is to copy them accurately from the law report.

■ Referring to statute

The source of some areas of law is statutory. For example, sticking with the example of a question about a manufacturer's liability for a faulty product, there is a statute on this subject, the Consumer Protection Act 1987, to which you would be expected to refer. This statute is discussed in Chapter 10. In the law of contract, while most contracts do not need to be expressed in writing, some do. The law on this is found in the Requirements of Writing (Scotland) Act 1995 which is discussed in Chapter 4.

The importance of reading

We hope that you will find this textbook helpful in your studies. Some colleges and universities may adopt it as the course textbook. However, you will be expected to read other material too, such as other textbooks and academic journal articles to support your learning. If you are studying at college or university, you will probably have received a reading list of useful material, in print and online, which should be available in the library. Note that nowadays universities and colleges subscribe to electronic databases, which may be available to you online. Legal databases include Westlaw, Lexis Nexis and Practical Law. It is useful to use these legal databases, if they are available to you, as they make sure that you have access to the latest versions of statutes and the latest cases. Students should never imagine that they will receive everything they need to learn in the course lectures and handouts. It is really important to read around the subject.

'Reading' nowadays is an outdated word, as all media can be useful and relevant: as well as newspapers and other print media useful audiovisual content can be found in You Tube videos and other podcasts, which are freely available on the internet. What makes the study of law exciting is when you make the link between what is happening in the news and the commercial law you are studying. You therefore need to keep up to date with the news, particularly about business.

One word of caution about using the internet in order to research the law: what you find on the internet can be of varying quality. Some material on the internet may be biased towards the point of view of the writer. Some material on the internet may also be written by inexperienced writers and the legal content may be inaccurate or not up-to-date. Please be careful that what you find is actually about the legal system you are studying and not a different one. If you are asked to write about the Scottish courts, while it might be easier to find material about the English or American courts, it is pointless to do so.

How to write about commercial law

We have already mentioned the need to give legal authority for every point you make about law.

■ Problem questions

In a course that might make use of this textbook, questions are often phrased in the form of problems (case studies), which lay out a set of facts, in which are embedded some legal problems. Often in these case studies there has been a problem with forming a contract, or a contract has been breached, or faulty products have injured customers, or an agent has taken a secret commission unknown to the principal. The task is:

1   to analyse the facts,
2   to identify the legal issues and
3   to apply relevant law to them.

Examples of this kind of question can be found in the review questions associated with most of the chapters of the book. This type of question is designed to enable you to display knowledge not only of what the law is but also how to apply it. This might involve thinking a bit about the implications of the facts, as perhaps the case law you know about does not exactly fit the scenario. Most of the facts in these scenarios will be relevant to the question, and they will usually bear some resemblance to cases with which you are familiar.

Tips for answering law questions in assessments

When writing about the law in assessments, here are some **dos** and **don'ts**:

DO

- take notice of all assessment guidance

- take time to make sure you understand the question

- make a plan if you find that helpful

- remember to give legal authority for all assertions about the law

- answer all parts of the question

- pay attention to any guidance about the breakdown of the marks

- manage your time carefully in an exam,

- try to present your work in a structured way

- write a full enough answer in the time limit to give yourself the best chance of getting a good mark

DON'T

- do a 'brain dump': **never** write about all you know, regardless of whether it is relevant; this wastes your time and may result in the deduction of marks

- write in bullet points,(except where you are running out of time in your final question)

- write extensively on the facts of cases: restrict yourself to discussion of the point of law decided in the case

■   Essay questions

The other main type of question you are likely to meet in assessments is the essay question. These will call for you to show you have some legal knowledge on the issue, but may also ask you to **discuss** the legal issues. You may be asked to **analyse** the issues, which involves breaking them down into their elements in order to understand them. You might be asked about some 'grey areas' where the law is unclear or the law may be in need of reform. However, the courses supported by this book would not normally demand a very high degree of critical analysis from a student, as courses supported by this book are usually undertaken at quite an early stage in one's studies, and many students will not have studied law previously.

Conclusion

People study law for different reasons and in different locations. The chapter gave an introduction to the study of commercial law in a global context, and explored the areas of law that will be discussed in more detail in the pages of this book. The chapter also provided guidance on how to study commercial law, particularly where your main subject of study is something other than law, and how to do well in assessments in the subject.

Further reading

Ashton, C., et al. (2012) *Understanding Scots Law: an Introduction to Scots Law, Procedure and Legal Skills.* 2nd revised ed., Edinburgh: W. Green. Chapter 18 (on legal skills, including doing coursework and exams).

Black, G., (ed) (2015) *Business Law in Scotland* 3rd ed., Edinburgh: W. Green, Chapter 1 pp 1-38, and Chapter 23 pp787-801.

ChartsBin: Legal Systems of the World. Available at: http://chartsbin.com/view/aq2 [Accessed 17 May 2016]. You can explore this interactive map to view the legal systems of the world to see which family of legal system each belongs to.

Grant, F., (2014) *Legal Research Skills for Scots Lawyers* 3rd ed., Edinburgh: W. Green Chapters 3, 5, 10, 13 and 14.

Higgins, E. and Tatham, L., (2015) *Successful Legal Writing* 3rd revised ed., London: Sweet & Maxwell.

Hodge, P., (2015) Does Scotland need its own commercial law? *Edinburgh Law Review,* **19** (1),299-310.

Juriglobe: World Legal Systems. Available at: http://www.juriglobe.ca/eng/sys-juri/index-syst.php

MacQueen, H., (2012) *Studying Scots Law* 4th ed. Edinburgh: Bloomsbury Professional. Chapter 1, 9, 10 and 12.

Office for National Statistics (2016) Overview of the UK Population: June 2016. Available at: https://www.ons.gov.uk/peoplepopulationandcommunity/populationandmigration/populationestimates [Accessed 24 July 2016]

2 Legal System of Scotland

Yvonne McLaren and Josephine Bisacre

This chapter discusses the formal sources of Scots law – answering the question of where the law gets its binding authority from. The chapter considers the role played by human rights in the Scottish legal system and their importance both for individuals and for businesses. While most commercial contracts are fulfilled and do not end up in court, some do, and sometimes businesses are sued for negligence, and they may also fall foul of the criminal law. Therefore the latter part of the chapter discusses the civil and criminal courts of Scotland and the personnel that work in the justice system. The Scottish legal system is also set in its UK and European context, and the chapter links closely with Chapters 3 and 4, where two rather different legal systems – those in Dubai and Malaysia – are explored, in order to provide some international comparisons.

The formal sources of Scots Law: from where does the law derive its authority?

What is the law and why should we obey it? These are important questions. Rules come in many different guises. There are legal rules and other rules that may appear similar in that they invoke a sense of obligation, such as religious rules, ethical or moral rules, and social rules. People live by religious or moral codes and consider themselves bound by them. People honour social engagements because personal relationships depend on this. However, legal rules are different in that the authority of the state is behind them and if they are not honoured, ultimately the state will step in and enforce them, in the form of civil remedies such as damages, or state-sanctioned punishment for breach of the criminal law.

All law comes from a formal source. The formal sources of Scots law have different levels of authority over us. Their order of importance is:

Legislation
Judicial precedent
The Institutional writers
Custom
Equity

■ Legislation

Legislation that is binding in Scotland can be enacted by various law-making institutions: it may be enacted by the European Union or by the UK or Scottish parliaments or by a body to which power to legislate has been delegated. The Crown also has residual legislative power.

There are four sources of legislation that are binding in Scotland. They are:

The European Union (EU)
The UK Parliament
The Scottish Parliament
The Royal Prerogative

Firstly, **European legislation**. The EU is made up of 28 member states (including the UK) covering four million square kilometres, stretching from Cyprus in the east to the Azores in the west, which are home to 503 million people. The EU affords certain important freedoms to its citizens.

The 'four freedoms' offered to EU citizens, including businesses

■ free movement of goods

■ free movement of workers

■ freedom of establishment and to provide services

■ free movement of capital

The EU is a free market, and its citizens can work in all the other member states and travel freely between them, and be treated without discrimination. Businesses are free to set up branches and form companies in other member states, and must be treated in the same way as local businesses. Many EU member states have a common currency, the Euro.

European legislation comes in various layers:

☐ **Treaties** are agreed between the member states, and create the rules for the European Community (now European Union). The first treaty was the Treaty of Rome in 1957, the most recent being the Lisbon Treaty in 2009.

☐ **Regulations** are laws made by the EU which are directly applicable to the citizens throughout the EU and do not have to be enacted into domestic law in order to be binding, for example the new general data protection regulation which has recently been agreed by the EU, and is expected to come into force in 2018.

☐ **Directives** are binding on member states as to the results to be achieved, but they have first to be enacted by member states into their laws – for example there are directives on health and safety, which have been enacted as statutes (acts of parliament) by the member states.

☐ There are also **decisions** which are binding on the parties to whom they are addressed; and finally

☐ **Recommendations** and **opinions** which have no binding force.

The member states of the EU have agreed that the EU should have legislative competence in certain areas only and within those areas all member states are bound by EU law, and can be taken to the European Court of Justice in Luxembourg if they do not comply. Much of EU law relates to the creation of the single European market, and to enabling free movement of workers. Examples of areas influenced to a greater or lesser extent by EU law are equality law, health and safety law, environmental law, consumer law, banking and financial law, intellectual property law, and company law. In its areas of application, European legislation is a more important source of law than statutes than come from national parliaments.

The second most authoritative source of law is **legislation from the UK parliament in London** in areas of law that apply across the UK, and acts of the Scottish parliament in their area of application. As well as acts of the UK parliament that apply UK-wide, there are many statutes (acts of parliament) that were passed by the parliament in London to apply specifically to Scotland, in the period before the Scottish parliament came into being. Examples that are covered in this book are the Age of Legal Capacity (Scotland) Act 1991 and the Requirements of Writing (Scotland) Act 1995. Many areas of statutory law apply throughout the UK such as the Human Rights Act 1998, the Companies Act 2006 and the Equality Act 2010. Acts of the UK parliament start their life as *bills*, which are put to both houses of parliament for consideration, (the House of Commons and the House of Lords). When a final text has been approved, the bill becomes an act of parliament, which is given the royal assent by the Queen, and it will come into force on a defined date. The parliament in London is a sovereign parliament, and has power to enact laws on any subject, even in areas where it has agreed to cede law-making competence to the European Union, (though it would normally choose not to do so). Areas of commercial law which are within the legislative competence of the UK parliament are employment law, health and safety law, and environmental law.

The Scottish parliament, which is based in Edinburgh, came into being in 1999. As discussed in Chapter 1, there had previously been a parliament in Scotland until it unified with the parliament in London in 1707. The modern Scottish parliament is not sovereign and has to legislate within the sphere of competence given to it by the Scotland Acts 1998 and 2012, and the latest Scotland Act 2016, much of which is not yet in force. If the Scottish parliament enacts legislation outside its powers, the legality of its legislation can be challenged. There is only one legislative chamber in this parliament. The Scottish parliament has authority to pass legislation in all areas not specifically reserved to the parliament in London, and they include the areas of law which were always different in Scotland such as contract, delict (in England tort), property law, criminal law, and family law.

There are also assemblies with devolved powers in Northern Ireland (Belfast) and Wales (Cardiff).

Delegated legislation, or secondary legislation, is created by other bodies under the authority of legislation from one of the parliaments. Much of this subordinate legislation comes from government departments. The important thing about this kind of legislation is that the powers are carefully defined and if the subordinate legislation goes beyond its powers (*ultra vires*), it can be challenged and struck down by a court as incompetent.

The Crown has limited legislative power through the royal prerogative. This is exercised in modern times by government ministers or on the advice of government ministers rather than by the Queen herself. These powers include powers to prorogue and dissolve parliament and some powers to pass subordinate legislation.

■ Judicial precedent

Judicial precedent is another important formal source of law. Much of Scots law is not written down in statute, but was developed by the courts over a long period of time. With judicial precedent, the formal source of the law comes from judges in previous cases. If the previous case was on the same point of law as the current case in point, and the previous case came from a higher court, the decision in the earlier case will be *binding* on the judge in the later case. This only applies to the point of law necessary to decide the earlier case (*ratio decidendi*). Any other things said by the judge will not be binding as being *obiter dicta* or things said by the way. Precedents in English cases, while they are never binding on Scottish courts, may be persuasive on Scottish courts, if the law is identical in both countries, for example a statute that applies across the UK. Basically, there is a hierarchy of courts, whereby appeal courts bind each other in order of importance and bind the courts of first instance in civil law and criminal law (vertical effect). There is also a horizontal effect as well, whereby courts may be bound by earlier decisions of the same court, or a court at the same level, though there is some dubiety as to how this applies in Scotland. The Supreme Court, unlike the previous House of Lords, has not stated explicitly it is free to depart from its previous decisions, but Practice Direction 3 from the Supreme Court refers to dicta from the Supreme Court that state that it considers that the rule set by the House of Lords has become part of the jurisprudence of appeals and would apply to the Supreme Court. The civil and criminal court structure in Scotland is examined later in this chapter.

Judicial precedent is a useful concept because it leads to like cases being treated alike, which makes a legal system more predictable. It also allows the courts to develop a legal concept slowly over time as society changes.

Most areas of law covered in this book have their formal source of law in judicial precedent: most of the law of contract, law of delict and law of agency comes from and is developed by, precedents. The case *Donoghue v Stevenson* 1932 S.C .(H.L.) 31 which established the point of law that manufacturers owe the ultimate consumers of their products a duty of care when manufacturing, has been followed in later cases in the lower courts and has been exported as a precedent to other common law jurisdictions abroad.

Exercise

Not every country recognises that judicial precedent can be binding. Think about the possible strengths and weaknesses of having a system of binding judicial precedent.

■ Institutional Writers

Another formal source of law that has a much reduced place in modern times is the work of the institutional writers. In the period before the Act of Union in 1707, academic lawyers from Scotland regularly travelled to continental European universities to study, and borrowed ideas from ancient Roman law and from the continental legal systems. The most influential of them was James Dalrymple, Viscount Stair, who wrote *The Institutions of the Law of Scotland* in 1681. There was a view at one time that these authoritative writings were actually the law (primary source), rather than writings about the law (secondary source). Over time, their influence has declined, as the law has moved on and new statutes and case law have replaced them as the formal source of law. No textbook in modern times, however influential, is ever viewed as being a formal source of law.

■ Custom

Custom is a minor source of law in Scotland nowadays. Historically, most legal systems developed from local custom that was respected in communities, but nowadays custom is rarely a formal source of law. For custom to be a formal source of law, it must meet these criteria:

☐ be regarded as representing the law over a very long period of time;

☐ be definite and certain;

☐ be fair and reasonable; and

☐ be consistent with legal principle.

■   ## Equity

In Scotland, unlike England, equity is a very minor formal source of Scots law. England once had a separate system of equity with different courts, which Scotland never had. In Scotland, the Court of Session and the High Court of Justiciary both have an extraordinary equitable jurisdiction called the *nobile officium* (noble office) to fill in the gaps in the law by providing a remedy if none is available. These powers are used sparingly.

2

Key Concept: Formal sources of Scots law

Every statement you make about law has to be backed by legal authority, which comes from one or other of the formal sources of law. It is important to remember this in all your assessments during your legal studies.

Human rights law and its relevance to commercial law

It should be noted that unlike most countries, the UK does not have a written constitution as such, though various parts of it have been written down over the centuries. Some countries have a bill of rights as part of their written constitution. While UK citizens have human rights, as will be seen, they were not provided in the form of a bill of rights.

After the Second World War and the consequent revelations about the concentration camps and other atrocities perpetrated in Nazi Germany and further afield, there was recognition that the world needed to acknowledge that human beings had inalienable human rights, including the right to life. The Universal Declaration of Human Rights was issued by the General Assembly of the United Nations in 1948. It has since been translated into 466 languages, emphasising its global reach. The Universal Declaration of Human Rights, though influential, is not legally binding on states, and many states do not recognise all of the rights in the Universal Declaration. In Europe, in order to create an instrument that would be binding on states in the continent of Europe, (at least if they chose to sign and ratify it) the European Declaration of Human Rights and Fundamental Freedoms was issued by the Council of Europe in 1950.

Convention rights that apply to the world of business:

■ The right to life (article 2)

■ The prohibition of torture and degrading treatment (article 3)

■ The prohibition of slavery (article 4)

■ The right to liberty and security (article 5)

■ The right to a fair trial (article 6)

■ The prohibition of torture without law behind it (article 7)

■ Respect for private and family life (article 8)

■ Freedom of expression (article 10)

■ Freedom from discrimination (article 14)

■ Right to peaceful enjoyment of possessions (article 1 of protocol 1)

■ Right to education (article 1 protocol 2), which must accord with the parents' religious and philosophical convictions.

The Council of Europe has 47 member states, including Turkey, Russia and Greenland, and is often wrongly confused with the European Union, which has 28. The EU member states are all members of the Council of Europe, but there are many more. The idea was that the convention should be enforceable against member states which denied these rights to citizens, and therefore a **European Court of Human Rights** was created, which sits at Strasbourg in France. Human rights cases can be brought by individuals and businesses, and are directed at states or organs of the state, for failure to respect human rights law in their own laws or their activities. Since 1966 UK citizens have been allowed to take cases of human rights abuse to that court, although it used to take about five years for cases to get to court. One leading case taken to that court from Scotland related to the use of corporal punishment in Scottish classrooms (*Campbell and Cousans v UK* judgment of 25 Feb 1982, Series A no 48, 4 EHRR 293, 40), which resulted in corporal punishment being banned in Scottish schools, since using the belt was found to represent a failure to respect the philosophical convictions of the child's parents with regard to education.

In 1998 the Human Rights Act was passed in the UK in order to allow recourse to the domestic courts in human rights cases against public bodies in the UK. The UK parliament is sovereign and therefore in theory could pass legislation that is contrary to human rights legislation, but if it did so, the UK could be found to be in breach of human rights law. It should be noted that Scottish legislation has to be compatible with human rights law, otherwise it cannot be passed. The Human Rights Act 1998 has been much used to challenge acts of the state, such as the failure of the Scottish prison service to install flushing toilets in prison cells: that had to change following a court challenge that asking prisoners to 'slop out' their cells constituted inhumane and degrading treatment contrary to Article 3 of the Convention. There have been various challenges to decisions of the government under immigration laws regarding deportation of non-UK nationals to regimes which practice torture. It should also be noted that the courts in judging cases in the UK have to respect human rights norms.

Businesses have been held to possess some of the Convention rights too, such as the right to a fair trial, freedom of expression and the right to peaceful enjoyment of property.

While businesses cannot be taken to court for abuses of human rights as such, their reputation is important to them, and negative publicity travels around the world very fast nowadays as we are all connected through smart phones and new media such as WhatsApp, Facebook and Twitter. Pictures of unacceptable sweatshops in developing countries in which cheap garments are made for businesses in developed countries will harm those companies' reputation and lose them customers. Conduct which breaches human rights may also breach criminal law or may give rise to a civil action for delict or for breaching property rights. For example, several lawsuits have been brought against Shell by Ogoni tribesmen in Nigeria who suffered dispossession of their land in the Niger Delta to make way for Shell's oil operations, and human rights abuses and pollution over many decades. One action brought by the Ogoni people in a New York court resulted in an out-of-court settlement of $15.5m in 2009 and Shell has now paid $83m in such settlements.

It should be said that there is some criticism in the UK about the precise content of the rights provided by the European convention, and recently there has been some discussion about enacting a bill of rights for the UK, making some changes to the content of the rights which currently apply, and this remains a possibility.

Overview of the Scottish Civil and the Scottish Criminal Justice Systems

It is important to be aware that the United Kingdom has three major legal systems, one in England and Wales, one in Northern Ireland and one in Scotland, and each has its own court structure and its own legal rules.

■ Differences between Civil and Criminal Law

Unlike its criminal counterpart, the civil justice system exists in order to resolve legal disputes between private individuals in a variety of areas including family law, company law, partnership law, the law of banking and finance, consumer law, personal injury claims and the law of trusts and succession.

It may be said that the main function of the civil justice system is to compensate the innocent party who has suffered a loss as a result of someone's wrongful actions (as determined by law).

Contrast this for example with criminal law which can be viewed as an attempt by the state to maintain law and order by punishing certain individuals who behave in a way that is considered criminal and anti-social.

When we talk of criminal law, we will see that the public prosecutor is required to prove that the accused is guilty of a crime known to the Law of Scotland and that the accused is guilty of a crime **beyond reasonable doubt**. Contrast this with the civil scenario where the parties are merely required to demonstrate that their version of the story has been decided by the judge/ jury to be true on the **balance of probabilities**. This may mean that a sheriff will decide in favour of one party over the other by preferring their version of the facts which he believes to be more accurate or more 'believable'.

One further advantage within the civil scenario is that corroboration or the ability to provide evidence or back-up proof, is not as strictly required as it is in criminal law, i.e. within the criminal law there is a very strict burden on the prosecutor that he be able to corroborate his evidence against the accused. Corroboration could come via the use of witnesses or increasingly via forensic evidence.

■ Procedure

When determining the difference between civil and criminal wrongs it may be said that the essential determining factor is one of legal procedure, i.e. if a legal wrong can be followed up by civil procedure it is a civil wrong and vice versa. Further if it can be pursued by both procedures, it is both a civil and criminal wrong. An example of this is fraud, which is both a criminal offence in Scotland and may give rise to an action in the law of delict brought by the victim of the fraud against the perpetrator.

We must therefore ask the question – what is the difference between civil and criminal procedure?

Essentially there are four main differences:

☐ The general essence of civil procedure is that it is initiated by the individual who has been wronged.

☐ Distinctive terminology is used in both civil and criminal procedure.

If the matter is civil and the matter reaches a court case, reference is made to the **pursuer** and the **defender**. If the pursuer is successful they are awarded a decree against the defender giving civil remedy. The defender is said to have been found liable.

In contrast the criminal terminology refers to the **prosecutor** or **the Crown prosecuting an accused.** If the case is successful the accused is found guilty and convicted giving rise the various sanctions the court may have within its power. If the prosecution fails, the accused is acquitted.

☐ The police tend not to be involved in civil procedure.

☐ Civil proceedings go to courts with civil jurisdiction and criminal proceedings go to courts with criminal jurisdiction.

Key Concept: the Civil and Criminal Justice Systems

The civil justice system is concerned with **remedies** to put right a wrong, while the criminal justice system is concerned with state-sanctioned **punishment** and rehabilitation in relation to conduct that the state wishes to eliminate from society

---

The Civil Justice System in Scotland

In describing the parties to a civil action we often refer to **litigants**. The parties to the action, or the litigants, are then divided up into firstly the **pursuer** i.e. the individual who brings the dispute to the attention of the court via the lodging of a legal action and secondly we have the **defender** in other words the individual or party against whom the legal action is being brought. It is worth mentioning that in English cases the equivalent terms are **claimant** (formerly **plaintiff**) and **defendant**.

Note

It is important to note that the state merely provides court facilities which parties to a private or civil dispute may use; people generally cannot be forced to use these civil courts if they do not want to.

The Civil Justice System consists of three main courts:

■ The sheriff court

The sheriff court is generally regarded as the busiest court within the Scottish System, since it deals with both criminal and civil matters. Since 1975 Scotland has been divided into six sheriffdoms. These are: Grampian, Highlands and Islands, Tayside, Central and Fife, Lothian and Borders, Glasgow and Strathkelvin, South Strathclyde, Dumfries and Galloway, and North Strathclyde.

Types of Actions which may be heard within the sheriff court:

These include small claims, summary procedure and ordinary procedure. Small claims are a relatively new form of procedure and were introduced in 1988 via The Small Claims (Scotland) Order 1988. Small claims are designed to be simpler and less formal and can only be applied for in the sheriff court.

As of the 1st January 2016, we now have a Sheriff Appeal Court which was established to deal with civil appeals. Further developments have also included a new Sheriff Personal Injury Court which is now opened in Edinburgh via The Courts Reform (Scotland) Act 2014.

■ The Court of Session

Historically the Lords of Council and Session had been a part of the King's Council but after receiving financial support from the Vatican in Rome, King James V established a separate institution, namely the College of Justice, or Court of Session, in 1532. The structure of the institution was based on the Parliament of Paris (an appellate court). The Court of Session is explicitly preserved "in all time coming" in Article XIX of The Treaty of Union between Scotland and England which was passed into legislation via The Acts of Union in 1706 and 1707.

The Court itself is designated as Scotland's Supreme Civil Court and sits in Parliament House in Edinburgh. It sits as a court of first instance and a court of appeal. The court is headed by the **Lord President** and the **Lord Justice Clerk**. Prospective litigants can now have some say in which judge they wish to hear their case. This may be useful if the lord/lady is known to have specialist expertise in that area.

The court is divided into the **Outer House** and the **Inner House**. The Outer House consists of 22 **lords ordinary** sitting alone or, in certain cases with a civil jury. The lords hear cases at first instance on a wide range of civil matters, including cases based on delict (tort) and contract, commercial cases and judicial review. The work of the judges covers a wide range, with certain designated judges dealing with intellectual property disputes. Special arrangements are made to deal with commercial cases. Please note that appeal lies in the first instance to the Inner House of the Court of Session and then to the Supreme Court of the United Kingdom.

The Inner House is essentially the appeal court, although it does have a small range of first instance business. The court is divided into the First and Second Divisions, of equal authority, and is presided over by the Lord President and the Lord Justice Clerk respectively. Each division is made up of six judges, but the quorum is three. The Divisions hear cases on appeal from the Outer House, the Sheriff Court Appeal Court and certain tribunals and other bodies. Occasionally, if a case is particularly important or difficult, or if it is necessary to overrule a previous binding authority, a larger court of five or more judges may be convened.

■ Personnel

Within the court, cases may be presented by:

- ☐ An advocate, who is a member of the Faculty of Advocates whose status and function correspond to that of a barrister in England,

- ☐ A solicitor-advocate, who is a member of the Law Society of Scotland, These legal personnel are generally experienced solicitors who obtain an extension of their rights of audience by undergoing additional training in evidence and in the procedure of the Court of Session,

- ☐ A practitioner from another member state of the European Union where the circumstances are prescribed by the European Communities (Service of Lawyers) Order 1978,

- ☐ An individual who is party to a case, but a firm or a company must always be represented by counsel or by a solicitor-advocate.

■ The UK Supreme Court

Formerly the highest court of civil appeal was the House of Lords. The creation of the new Supreme Court means that the most senior judges are now entirely separate from the Parliamentary process. The Constitutional Reform Act 2005 made provision for the creation of a new Supreme Court for the United Kingdom. There had, in recent years, been mounting calls for the creation of a new free-standing Supreme Court separating the highest appeal court from the second house of Parliament, and removing the Lords of Appeal in Ordinary from the legislature. On 12 June 2003 the Government announced its intention to do so.

In October 2009, The Supreme Court replaced the Appellate Committee of the House of Lords as the highest court in the United Kingdom.

The Court hears appeals on arguable points of law of the greatest public importance, for the whole of the United Kingdom in civil cases, and for England, Wales and Northern Ireland in criminal cases.

The Supreme Court sits in the former Middlesex Guildhall, on the western side of Parliament Square in London. This new location is highly symbolic of the United Kingdom's separation of powers, balancing judiciary and legislature across the open space of Parliament Square, with the other two sides occupied by the executive (the Treasury building) and the church (Westminster Abbey).

The Supreme Court also decides devolution issues under the Scotland Act 1998, the Northern Ireland Act 1998 and the Government of Wales Act 2006. These are issues about whether the devolved executive and legislative authorities in Scotland, Wales and Northern Ireland have acted or propose to act within their powers or have failed to comply with any other duty imposed on them. Devolution cases can reach the Supreme Court in three ways:

☐ Through a reference from someone who can exercise relevant statutory powers such as the Attorney General, whether or not the issue is the subject of litigation

☐ Through an appeal from certain higher courts in England and Wales, Scotland and Northern Ireland

☐ Through a reference from certain appellate courts.

The Supreme Court, as well as being the final court of appeal, plays an important role in the development of United Kingdom law. As an appeal court, the Supreme Court cannot consider a case unless a relevant order has been made in a lower court.

The Supreme Court hears appeals from the following courts in each jurisdiction:

☐ **England and Wales:** The Court of Appeal, Civil Division, the Court of Appeal, Criminal Division and (in some limited cases) the High Court.

☐ **Scotland:** The Court of Session.

☐ **Northern Ireland:** The Court of Appeal in Northern Ireland, (in some limited cases) the High Court.

The Criminal Justice System

It may be argued that criminal law is a reflection of the values that a society or community currently holds, i.e. who knows what the future holds?

In the past, certain activities would almost certainly be considered a criminal act, for example being a member of an independent trade union, would have been regarded as a criminal act under the Combination Acts, the penalty for which may have been transportation overseas to Australia, in those days regarded as a harsh penal colony. It might be suggested that values and attitudes have changed, but there are, however, certain types of behaviour, e.g. murder, assault, sexual offences, theft and criminal damage which have consistently remained forbidden by law.

■ The participants

In criminal law the individual on trial is referred to as the **accused** (or the **panel**). In Scots Law, it is a fundamental principle that the accused on trial be considered innocent until proven guilty. (Please note the power of the Lord Advocate to intervene, for example where any undue amount of press coverage may hinder the rights of the accused).

In other words, it is for the public prosecutor to prove beyond reasonable doubt that the accused is guilty of crime known to the Law of Scotland.

This gives the prosecution the strict burden that they must be able to corroborate any evidence being used against the accused. Corroboration here is generally via the testimony of witnesses and increasingly via the use of expert and forensic evidence. In Scotland the public prosecution of a crime is within the responsibility of the Lord Advocate. All prosecutions in Scotland are done by the state, except in rare cases where permission for a private prosecution is granted. The Lord Advocate is the most senior law officer in the Crown Office. Prosecution in the lower courts is done by the Procurator Fiscal service.

The Scottish criminal courts have three possible verdicts: guilty, not guilty and not proven. The not proven verdict is currently being reviewed and may be scrapped. The English criminal courts do not have the not proven verdict. If the accused is found guilty, he/she will be sentenced. Typically this would be a fine and/or a jail sentence.

The Criminal Justice System consists of three main courts:

■ Justice of the Peace Court

These courts are a unique part of Scotland's criminal justice system. They courts have replaced the District Courts which were established in 1975 under local authority administration. The Justice of the Peace courts are administered, along with the other courts, by the Scottish Courts and Tribunals Service.

A justice of the peace is a lay magistrate, appointed from within the local community and trained in criminal law and procedure. They sit either alone, or in a bench of three, and deal with the less serious summary crimes, such as speeding, careless driving and breach of the peace. In court, justices have access to advice on the law and procedure from lawyers, who fulfil the role of legal advisers or clerk of court. A justice of the peace court can be presided over by a stipendiary magistrate who is a legally qualified solicitor or advocate who sits alone. They deal with more serious business similar to sheriffs, such as drink driving, dangerous driving and assault.

■ The sheriff court

The sheriff's jurisdiction is very wide and varied and mainly original, i.e. not appellate. Much of the business of the sheriff court takes the form of summary trials, but it also has solemn jurisdiction. It is said to be the most important of the lower criminal courts.

The sheriff court has jurisdiction over all crime committed in the sheriff court district other than crown pleas, i.e. those reserved for the High Court of Justiciary: murder, rape, treason and serious drug offences. Prosecution is by the procurator fiscal, the exercise of whose discretion to prosecute follows a report from the police and is subject to the supervision of the lord advocate and the crown office. The procurator fiscal's choice of court and procedure to be followed (solemn with a jury or summary) depends on the seriousness of the case and the sentence he expects the court to pass.

There are limits to the sentencing powers of the sheriff, which may lead the prosecutor to bring the case before the High Court of Justiciary. The maximum fine may be unlimited where the sheriff sits with a jury of fifteen and up to five years of imprisonment may be administered.

We now have a new Sheriff Appeal Court, established via the Courts Reform (Scotland) Act 2014. It hears appeals against summary criminal proceedings from both the sheriff and justice of the peace courts. The Bench will generally be composed of two or three appeal sheriffs depending on the type of appeal to be considered. The court is currently based in Edinburgh and will normally be presided over by a single appeal sheriff.

■   ## The High Court of Justiciary

Established in 1672 this court comprises the Lord Justice-General, the Lord Justice-Clerk and all other judges of the Court of Session (Lord Commissioners of Justiciary). The High Court of Justiciary is Scotland's supreme criminal court. When sitting as a court of first instance as a trial court, it hears the most serious criminal cases. A single judge hears cases with a jury of fifteen lay people.

The High Court may deal with all nature of crimes, but it has exclusive jurisdiction over the most serious crimes, e.g. rape, murder, treason and serious drug offences. Proceedings are conducted by the Lord Advocate (in whose name all prosecutions are brought in the public interest) or the Solicitor-General, his deputy, but generally on a day-to-day basis it will be done by an Advocate-Depute (state prosecutor). Its jurisdiction extends to the whole of Scotland, including its territorial waters, and outside Scotland in relation to murder or culpable homicide by a Scottish subject.

Generally the defence will be conducted by an advocate or solicitor-advocate. As previously stated advocates are members of the Faculty of Advocates and have a status and function corresponding to that of a barrister in England. Advocates previously had an exclusive right of audience in the High Court but since 1990, they now share this right with solicitor-advocates who are members of the Law Society of Scotland. Please note that an accused may conduct their own defence in certain types of cases.

When sitting as an appeal court, the court consists of at least three judges when hearing appeals against conviction and two when hearing sentence appeals. It is also possible for more judges to sit when the court is dealing with exceptionally difficult cases or those where important matters of law may be considered.

In terms of sentencing, the maximum penalties which the high court may impose include life imprisonment for certain common law crimes, e.g. murder. For the parties involved the general rule is that the persons shall be prosecuted in the courts where they are domiciled, which may be defined as the place with which they have the greatest connection.

Exercise

Bill persuaded his bank to lend his £10,000, having given the bank forged evidence to prove his ability to pay. The bank is seeking to recover the loan, which Bill has since spent.

Discuss how the civil and criminal courts might be used in this case, and the different outcomes that arise in these two sets of courts.

Conclusion

The purpose of this chapter, along with Chapter 1, is to set the legal scene for what will be discussed in the rest of the book: it looked at what gives the law its binding force, the formal sources of Scots law, and what happens when disputes fetch up in court or businesses are prosecuted for breach of the criminal law. It also explored the importance of human rights law as an important protection for individuals and for businesses. In Chapters 3 and 4, some parallels and some distinctions will be drawn between Scots law and two exemplar jurisdictions, the United Arab Emirates and Malaysia.

Further reading

Black, G.,(ed) (2015) *Business Law in Scotland* 3rd edition Edinburgh: W Green Chapters 1 and 2.European Convention on Human Rights http://www.echr.coe. int/documents/convention_ENG.pdf [accessed 11.04.2016]

European Union web-site http://europa.eu [accessed 11.04.2016]

Globalglasgow (2014) Scottish Criminal Justice System Part 1 https://www.youtube. com/watch?v=4xaKAgx_Uw4 [accessed 11.04.2016]. Note there are three further videos on this subject, parts 2-4.

Guthrie, T., (2016) The Scottish Legal System and Sources of Law https://www. youtube.com/watch?v=IYA3JQO3crM [accessed 11.04.2016]

Judiciary of Scotland http://www.scotland-judiciary.org.uk/16/0/Court-Structure [accessed 11.04.2016]

Scottish Courts and Tribunals http://www.scotcourts.gov.uk [accessed 11.04.2016]

Scottish Parliament web-site http://www.scottish.parliament.uk [accessed 11.04.2016]

Shiels, R., (2015) *Law Basics: Scottish Legal System* 4th ed Edinburgh: W. Green.

UK Parliament web-site http://www.parliament.uk [accessed 11.03.2016]

White, R, Willock, I., and MacQueen, H., (2013) *The Scottish Legal System* 5th ed , Haywards Heath: Bloomsbury Professional, Chapters 2 and 5.

3 The UAE Legal System

Zeenat Beebeejaun

The United Arab Emirates, also known as the UAE, is commonly referred to as the business hub of the region, with numerous business entities setting up their headquarters or their branches there, to enable a more effective way of trading with the Persian Gulf countries as well as the Far East.

Its federal laws emanate from its Constitution, which is the main political and legal framework enabling the United Arab Emirates to operate as a federation of the seven emirates.

The focus of this chapter is similar to that of Chapter 2 and Chapter 4: the constitutional basis of the legal system, the way the legislature works in the UAE, and the court system are explored. It also discusses the Dubai International Financial Centre, which departs in some ways from the legal systems in the UAE, in adopting laws that focus particularly on the needs of international business.

The UAE constitution

■ History

Prior to 1971, what is now the United Arab Emirates was a British protectorate – the British Residency of the Persian Gulf. In 1971, a temporary constitution was formed which enshrined the legal and political framework of the United Arab Emirates, also referred to as 'The Union'. This union is commemorated as the UAE National Day on 2nd December each year which celebrates its formal independence as a federal state and which encourages the feeling of unity and common beliefs across the seven emirates.

The Union was originally comprised of six emirates namely Abu Dhabi, Dubai, Sharjah, Ajman, Fujairah and Umm Al Quwain. The emirate of Ras

Al Khaimah became the seventh and last emirate to formally join the federation in 1972. The capital of the UAE is Abu Dhabi.

With the development of an increasingly integrated economy marked especially by free trade and free flow of capital, together with providing the world with a booming and modernised port, the UAE was compelled to develop its legal infrastructure thereby enabling traders to have a tangible legal jurisdiction to abide by in the event of any dispute.

Unlike the UK, the UAE has a written constitution. In 1996, the constitution earned its permanent status and that year also marked the creation of a unified military and legal system. However, this was initially strongly opposed by the emirates of Dubai and Ras Al Khaimah, which until today have their own separate judicial systems with their own laws enacted by their respective rulers in areas where federal law is silent or absent.

■ Preamble, parts and articles of the Constitution

The preamble illustrates the motives behind the Union of the emirates which essentially revolve around establishing peace, unity and obtaining a stronger international presence in view of the upcoming globalization.

There are 10 parts in the UAE Constitution namely;

1 The Union, its fundamental constituents and aims

2 The Fundamental social and economic bases of the Union

3 Freedom, rights and public duties

4 The union authorities

5 Union legislation and decrees and the authorities having jurisdiction therein

6 The emirates

7 The distribution of legislative, executive and international jurisdiction between the union and the emirates

8 The financial affairs of the union

9 The armed forces and the security forces

10 Final and transitional provisions

These parts are further subcategorized into 151 articles with their main purpose being to encapsulate the various unanimous undertakings of the seven rulers from the seven emirates.

Articles 2, 3 and 10 of Part 1 of the constitution are particularly note-worthy since they enshrine the desire for the United Arab Emirates to be a sovereign nation. This meant that each of the six emirates (initially it was the six rulers since Ras Al Khaimah joined in 1972) were prepared to observe a reciprocal recognition of the other territories, populations and customs whilst also being governed by federal legislation enacted by the Federal Supreme Council.

■ The Federal Supreme Council

The Federal Supreme Council which is also known as the Supreme Council of the Union was established by Article 45 of the Constitution which also stipulated, in addition, that the union will consist of –

□ The President of the Union and his Deputy

□ The Council of Ministers of the Union

□ The Union National Council

□ The Union Judiciary

Articles 46 and 47 further entitle the Federal Supreme Council to enjoy supreme law-making powers whilst also being viewed as the highest con-stitutional authority, thereby formulating general policies on all matters related to the union and other matters that would contribute to the achieve-ment of the motives behind the union of the emirates.

The Federal Supreme Council is the body responsible for the sanctioning of decrees on matters that are subject to ratification and which require its approval. Amidst several supreme powers, it is also vested with the power of appointing the Chairman of the Council of Ministers of the Union as well as his resignation and the appointment of the President and the judges of the Supreme Union Court as well as their resignation or dismissal.

Formal sources of law

■ An overview of the various sources of law in the UAE

Despite the fact that the core principles of law in the UAE are derived from Shari'a, most of its legislation is comprised of a mixture of concepts from civil law jurisdictions and in particular it was strongly influenced by Egyptian legal codes, which in turn were influenced by French law.

Bearing in mind that the UAE is a civil law jurisdiction, (see Chapter 1) its only sources of law are codified within the federal laws and decrees which serve as the primary source of law.

Furthermore, the UAE Constitution stipulates the basic principles and undertakings of the Union from which federal laws emanate. As such, it has given powers to:

☐ the Supreme Council of the Union to ratify various Union laws (federal laws) and decrees.

☐ the President of the Union to sign the Union laws which the Supreme Council has ratified.

☐ the Council of Ministers to propose draft Union laws which are initially sent to the Union National Council before they are submitted to the President of the Union.

Chapter 5 of the Constitution illustrates the procedures by which Union laws are passed. Once the law has been signed by the President of the Union, it is published in the Official Gazette of the Union within a maximum of two weeks from the date of signature and promulgation by the President of the Union after the Supreme Council has ratified it.

Such law then becomes effective one month after its publication in the Official Gazette unless another date has been stipulated within the law itself.

■ Local laws

As mentioned earlier, the Constitution has bestowed upon the member emirates the power to have their own legislative body which would be responsible to enact local laws and decrees in areas whereby federal laws are absent, provided they are in accordance with the Constitution. Therefore, despite the fact that the rulers of each emirate had opted to surrender some of their sovereign prerogatives to form the Union, they retained some aspects of sovereignty at an emirate level.

Article 3 of the Constitution further depicts the aspect of residual sovereignty by stating that *"the member emirates shall exercise sovereignty over their own territories and residual waters in all matters which are not within the jurisdiction of the Union as assigned by the Constitution."*

However, it is important to note Article 99 of the Constitution which gives additional weight to federal laws by stating that *"...the constitutionality of legislation promulgated by one of the emirates shall be examined by the Supreme Court if they are challenged by one of the emirates on the grounds of violation of the Constitution of the Union or Union laws."*

As such, the emirates do have some power to legislate their local laws bearing in mind that such laws should go in line with the essence of the Constitution and therefore should be Shari'a compliant to some extent.

The Constitution has however reserved to the Union absolute power on matters such as the declaration of martial law, the elimination of taxes and internal tariffs, the formation of unified armed forces and the right to form federal security forces, amongst others.

Having adopted the civil law system, the UAE like many other countries, rely heavily on codified laws as the main source of legislation. Since Shari'a is part of the backbone upon which the UAE legal system has coalesced, some of the Islamic principles are now embedded within its legal framework, one of them being a well established principle whereby discretionary interpretation is not allowed in matters covered by specific legislation. Therefore, judicial precedents are not construed as being part of the legislative framework but can be persuasive and can be used as an indicator to the interpretation of a specific law.

■ Shari'a as a source of law

Whilst there is a misapprehension of Shari'a law shared by many around the world, Islamic Law covers all branches of today's modern law and every domain of human activity, either at individual level, society level or within the international domain. As such, Islamic Law encompasses niche areas such as Constitutional Law, Administrative Law, Criminal Law and Commercial Law as well as Devotional Law and Personal Law, amongst many other areas of law which go beyond the scope of this chapter.

Shari'a law is the law of Islam and it is based upon the actions and words of Prophet Muhammad (S.A.W.) which are called '*Sunnah*' and the Quran. Although Shari'a law cannot be altered, its interpretation called '*fiqh*' by Islamic jurists, is given some leeway. Four main schools of thought have emanated through the passage of time which were led by four knowledgeable jurists who tried to systemise the Islamic Law into a comprehensive system covering most legal situations. Most Muslims regard these four schools as demonstrating equally valid interpretations of the religious law of Islam but the difference is highlighted by their interpretations and reasoning on areas where the Quran is silent.

As Article 7 of the UAE Constitution states that "…*the Islamic Shari'a shall be a principal source or legislation in the Union…*" it can be argued that the UAE laws can utilise other sources whilst drafting its laws, if required. As such, Article 1 of the UAE Civil Code issued as Federal Law No.5 of 1985 which is the basic law of the UAE states that "*..if the judge finds no provision in this law, he has to pass judgement in accordance to Shari'a law…*" which makes it apparent that where UAE law contains a specific provision, the UAE courts will give effect to that provision. However, Article 2 of the UAE Civil Code also states that the rules and principles of Islamic jurisprudence shall be relied upon in the understanding and interpretations of provisions of law which again narrows our understanding to the fact that Shari'a law has a great impact on the UAE laws.

Exercise

Compare the formal sources of law in the UK covered in Chapter 2 with those of the UAE: what are the similarities and differences?

The UAE court structure

■ Overview of the UAE courts

The judiciary has been independent from the time of the Union and that is enshrined within article 94 of the UAE constitution. Bearing in mind that the UAE is a sovereign nation affiliated to a federal system which consists of a central authority governing the emirates, it is noteworthy to mention that the Constitution also permits each member emirate to establish its own local courts in which local disputes can be heard.

However, Article 99 of the UAE constitution reserves the right to the Federal Supreme Court (also known as the Supreme Union Court) to adjudicate on matters such as disputes between the member emirates, the constitutionality of a federal law, laws or regulations in general, criminal cases that affect the interests of the UAE (forgery of official documents, crimes that relate to internal and external security, counterfeiting of currency) and claims of conflict of jurisdiction between a federal court and the court of an emirate.

In addition to the Constitution, the UAE Civil Procedures Law also establishes and reiterates on matters such as the jurisdiction of the federal courts which are part of the UAE Federal Judicial Authority as well as those that have incorporated their own legal systems within the UAE legal system.

As mentioned earlier, the Constitution allows each emirate to have its own legislative body and judicial authority and it is important to note that the only two emirates that have opted to have their own courts and legislatures are the emirates of Dubai and Ras Al Khaimah. As such, they are entitled to apply their laws (provided they are in accordance with the UAE Constitution) on matters on which the federal laws are silent: however, federal laws override the local emirate laws on all other areas.

3

■ The UAE Federal courts structure

```
┌─────────────────────────────┐
│   Federal Supreme Court     │
└─────────────────────────────┘

┌─────────────────────────────┐
│     Courts of Appeal        │
└─────────────────────────────┘

┌─────────────────────────────┐
│  Courts of First Instance   │
└─────────────────────────────┘
```

The illustration above depicts the federal court hierarchy in the UAE whereby the Federal Supreme Court, also known colloquially as the Court of Cassation, is the final Court of Appeal and is located in Abu Dhabi. Appeals from the Courts of First Instance will be on either points of fact or issues of law whilst any appeal against a Court of Appeal's decision will be on issues of law only. Since the UAE is a civil law jurisdiction, the system of precedence does not apply as opposed to common law jurisdictions such as England and Wales whereby the doctrine of precedent is prevalent and binding. As such, since the judges are only bound to follow the codified federal laws enacted by the Federal Supreme Council, the outcome of each case is fairly certain.

Exercise

Which emirat es have incorporated their judicial systems into the Federal system?

■ The Court Structure of the Emirate of Dubai

Court of Cassation

Court of Appeal

Court of First Instance

As the illustration depicts, Dubai enjoys a three-tiered judicial system whereby the Court of First Instance is the initial stage for most cases. Each court has a civil division, a criminal division and a Shari'a division with the latter hearing cases on civil matters such as divorce, child custody, inheritance and guardianship of minors between Muslims. Non Muslims are not subject to the Shari'a courts on any matter being in dispute.

An appeal against a decision of the Court of First Instance is to be made within 30 days of the judgement to the Court of Appeal. Such an appeal can be on a point of fact or an issue of law. However, an appeal against a Court of Appeal decision can only be on a point of law to the Court of Cassation. The appellant has a 30-day period to appeal from the date of judgement.

In accordance to Articles 158-168 of Civil Procedures Law No 11 of 1992, the appellant may appeal to the Court of Appeal provided that the sum in dispute is 20,000 Dirhams or more. However, the Court of Cassation has an appellate jurisdiction over disputes of 200,000 Dirhams and above only.

Each circuit (division) in the Court of Appeal is comprised of three judges with one of them being the presiding judge, while each circuit in the Court of Cassation is comprised of five judges, one known as the superior judge.

Dubai International Financial Centre ('DIFC')

■ Overview

The DIFC was part of the emirate of Dubai's infrastructure to attract capital and investment in the region. As defined by Federal Law No. 8 of 2004, it is a financial free zone having an independent jurisdiction within the UAE which is exempted from all federal civil and commercial laws with the exception of federal criminal laws. As such, it has been given the power of creating its own legal and regulatory framework.

In addition to the above, Dubai Law No. 9 of 2004 and Dubai Law No. 12 of 2004 acknowledge the creation of the DIFC and recognise its financial and administrative and judicial independence as well as its exemption from Dubai laws under certain conditions as stipulated therein. In a successful attempt to create an optimal environment offering businesses an opportunity to thrive, the DIFC's legal framework and court structure are modelled closely on the principles of common law.

There are other free zones across the various emirates.

3

■ DIFC legal framework and court structure

In order to create the DIFC and DIFC courts, an amendment had to be made to the UAE Constitution, which deals with the separation of powers between federal and local authorities, to allow the enactment of a financial free zone law. As a result of this, coupled with a federal decree recognising the DIFC as a financial free zone (Federal Decree No. 35 of 2004) and Dubai laws as mentioned above, DIFC Law No. 10 of 2004 (DIFC Court Law) was passed, which provided for the independent administration of justice within the DIFC. The DIFC Court Law enables the appointment of judges to the DIFC courts which operate as a two-tiered system, namely the Court of First Instance and the Court of Appeal.

The Court of First Instance is comprised of a single judge having exclusive jurisdiction over civil and/or commercial disputes within the DIFC jurisdiction or civil and/or commercial disputes involving the DIFC or its establishments and objections filed against a decision made by a DIFC body, which are subject to objection in accordance to DIFC laws and regulations.

The Court of Appeal is comprised of at least three judges with the Chief Justice or most senior judge presiding having exclusive jurisdiction over appeals made against judgements held by the Court of First Instance and interpretation of the DIFC laws as requested by DIFC bodies or establishments provided that such establishment has obtained leave of the Chief Justice.

DIFC laws range from company law to insolvency to employment and real property amidst other areas. They are attractive for foreign investors, as they permit 100% foreign ownership of companies which is not permitted outside the free zone, and there is no restriction on the repatriation of capital and profits of companies to the countries where shareholders are based.

Exercise

To what extent is the DIFC legal framework similar to that of the UK?

Conclusion

The chapter explored the main features of the legal system of the UAE, with reference also to the rather different legal regime that applies in the Financial Free Zone in Dubai. The UAE makes an interesting comparator to the UK, because of its fairly recent history as a British Protectorate, after which it has followed a different path, and its legal sytem is in the civil law tradition rather than the common law tradition. Shari'a law also has an important role to play in the legal system of the UAE in relation to their Moslem populations.

References

Carballo, A., (2007) The law of the Dubai international free zone: common law oasis or mirage within the UAE? *Arab Law Quarterly* **21**(1) 91-104.

Constitution of United Arab Emirates. Available at www.constituteproject.org/constitution/United_Arab_Emirates_2004.pdf [Accessed 20 May 2016].

Dubai Courts History and Structure. Available at www.dubaicourts.gov.ae [Accessed 20 May 2016].

Dubai International Financial Centre. Available at www.difc.ae [Accessed 20 May 2016].

Kedr, A and Alnuaimi, B (2010) A guide to the United Arab Emirates legal system. Available at www.nyulawglobal.org/globalex/United_Arab_Emirates.html [Accessed 20 May 2016].

Sabah M A Mahmoud (2014) UAE Company Law and Practice. Available at www.gulf-law.com [Accessed 20 May 2016]

UAE Free Zones. Available at www.uaefreezones.com [Accessed 20 May 2016].

UAEinteract. Setting up business. Available at www.uaeinteract.com/business/settingup.asp [Accessed 20 May 2016].

UAE Trade and Commercial Office. Doing Business in the UAE. Available at www.uaetrade-usa.org/index.php?page=economiy/ecmid=105 [Accessed 20 May 2016].

4 The Legal System of Malaysia

Bahma Sivasubramaniam

Like many Commonwealth countries, Malaysia inherited its political, legal and administrative systems from England. To a large extent therefore, there are many similarities between the legal systems of both these countries. Malaysia practises a parliamentary democracy and has a constitutional monarchy, just as the United Kingdom. The principal law-making body is Parliament. The Government is comprised of three arms: the Legislature, the Executive and the Judiciary, in common with other parliamentary democracies such as the United Kingdom.

In Chapter 2 and Chapter 3 we explored the Scottish legal system and that of the United Arab Emirates. This chapter will focus on the Malaysian legal system, in particular the sources of law and the structure and the hierarchy of the courts.

Role of history and geography on current legal system

Malaysia became independent in 1957, part of the country, Malaya, having previously been a British protectorate. The law prevalent in Malaysia comprises of local laws and laws of England received into the Malaysian Legal System through the doctrine of reception. This doctrine alludes to the practice whereby a former colony of England consciously and willingly adopts its laws (Rheinstein, M, 1956). Malaysia has also adopted its criminal laws from India and its land laws from Australia, both of which are Commonwealth countries. From this it can be seen that the Malaysian legal system belongs in large part to the common law family of legal systems discussed in Chapter 1.

It should be noted that Malaysia is geographically divided into two. The first part is what is known as the Peninsular Malaysia, comprising of eleven States and two Federal Territories. It is where the capital of the country is and is the seat of the Federal Parliament. East Malaysia, which is in the Borneo subcontinent across the South China Sea, is made up of Sabah, Sarawak and the Federal Territory of Labuan. Although the differences of the legal systems in Peninsular Malaysia and East Malaysia are not substantial, both parts have their own courts. They do however have the Supreme Court and the Court of Appeal in common. For the purposes of this chapter, the focus will be on the system as applied and practised in Peninsular Malaysia unless otherwise stated.

Formal sources of law

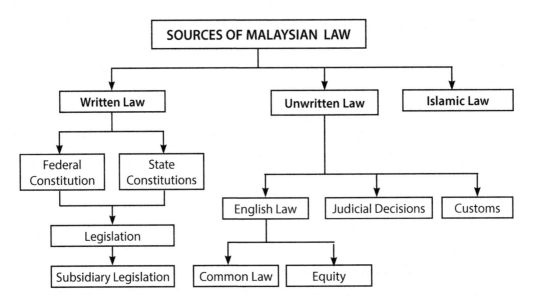

Figure 4.1: Formal sources of law

Sources of law insofar as relevant to this chapter simply mean where law originates from. These include constitutions, legislation, judgments of courts and secondary sources such as practice, customs, and tradition. Islamic Law is another source of law. Thus the laws in Malaysia may be categorised into three main groups: written, unwritten, and Islamic laws.

■ Written Law

Written laws are laws that are contained in formal instruments such as Constitutions and Legislation. The primary source of written law in the country is the Federal Constitution. State Constitutions too are sources of written law in Malaysia.

☐ Federal Constitution

The Federal Constitution of Malaysia is the foremost legal instrument and contains 181 provisions, called Articles. These Articles cover a myriad of issues such as the structures of the Federal and State Governments, the legislative powers of Parliament and State Legislative Assemblies, the fundamental rights of the individual, the jurisdiction of the superior courts and many more.

4

The Federal Constitution is the **supreme law** of the land. Any law passed must be consistent with the Federal Constitution.

Article 4 states:

Supreme Law of the Federation

This Constitution is the supreme law of the Federation and any law passed after Merdeka Day* which is inconsistent with this Constitution, shall to the extent of the inconsistency be void.

Merdeka Day – Independence Day – 31ˢᵗ August 1957

The powers of Parliament to legislate are contained within the parameters of the Federal Constitution. Its powers to legislate are not unfettered. Should Parliament pass any law that is *ultra vires* (beyond its powers) under the Federal Constitution, it can be challenged in a court of law. Should the court find that the challenged Act is unconstitutional, that Act (or parts of it as the case may be) can be struck down. Unlike the United Kingdom parliament, the doctrine of parliamentary supremacy is not applicable in Malaysia. In the case of *AJ Thian v Government of Malaysia [1976] 2 M.L.J. 112, 113* the Lord President (as the Head of Judiciary was then known) Tun Suffian had this to say:

"The doctrine of supremacy of Parliament does not apply to Malaysia. Here we have a written constitution. The power of Parliament and State Legislatures in Malaysia is limited by the Constitution and they cannot make any law as they please."

Acts of Parliament therefore must not contravene Article 4. Thus in *Repco Holdings v Government of Malaysia* (1997) 3 M.L.J. 681, the Court of Appeal held that by virtue of Article 4(1) of the Federal Constitution, any law passed by Parliament which is inconsistent with the Constitution shall be void.

Gopal Sri Ram JCA succinctly put it thus:

"Our Federal Constitution is a living document written for all time. Its language compresses within it ideas that are manifold and concepts which are multifaceted…..an Act of Parliament (that) contains provisions that are in direct conflict with the supreme law, it is the duty of this court to say so clearly and unequivocally."

Exercise 1

The constitution of Malaysia contains provisions granting fundamental liberties to the people. Article 6(1) of the Federal Constitution states: "No person should be held in slavery."The Parliament of Malaysia passes a law called Employment (Slavery) Act 2016 that states all manual workers earning MYR 900.00 or less a month shall be designated as slaves for tax purposes. Rose, a domestic help earning a monthly income of MYR 800,00, is now designated as a slave. Advise Rose. Your advice should be supported by statutory provisions and case law where necessary and relevant.

☐ State Constitutions

Each state in Malaysia has its own constitution. There are therefore 13 State Constitutions. Article 74 of the Federal Constitution sets out three lists: the Federal List, the State List and the Concurrent List. The Federal List sets out all matters that fall within the jurisdiction of the Federal Government. These include external affairs, national defence, internal security, citizenship and so on. The State List sets out matters that fall within the purview of the State Government. These are Islamic law, land, agricultural and forestry matters. The Third List is known as the Concurrent List. This List covers matters which fall within the jurisdiction between both the Federal and the State Governments.

Insofar as the State Constitution is concerned, it should not be inconsistent with the Federal Constitution. Any provisions which are in contradiction with the Federal Constitution are therefore void.

Exercise 2

Refer to Exercise 1

The Legislative Assembly of the State of Pahang defies Parliament and passes a law stating that slavery is unlawful. Advise the Legislative Assembly on the legality of its actions.

☐   **Legislation**

a. Primary Legislation (*Parent Legislation*)

4

Parliament is responsible for the enactment of primary legislation. It is based on the Westminster model, and hence is bicameral, made up of the Dewan Rakyat (the House of Commons equivalent) and the Dewan Negara (Senate equivalent). Legislation is identifiable by the word Act, such as the Computer Crimes Act 1997, Contracts Act 1950, Personal Data Protection Act 2010 and so on. 'Act of Parliament', 'statute' and 'legislation' are words that are used interchangeably to describe laws passed by Parliament. The provisions contained in an Act of Parliament are usually called Sections.

As stated above, the Malaysian Parliament cannot make any law it likes. It cannot pass laws that contravene the Federal Constitution. In *Repco (supra)*, the Court of Appeal struck out S.129(2) of the Securities Industry Act 1983 and s 39(2) of the Securities Commission Act 1993 as unconstitutional, null and void as they contravened the Federal Constitution.

States too are empowered to legislate on matters set out in the State List in the Federal Constitution. Generally speaking, the courts have stressed that there should be a harmony between federal laws and state laws. However, where there is a conflict between them, federal law prevails: Article 75. See also the case of *City Council of Georgetown and Anor v Government of the State of Penang and Anor* (1967) 1 MLJ 169 where the Federal Court held that a state law was void by virtue of its inconsistency with federal law.

b. Subsidiary Legislation (*delegated or subordinate legislation*)

Subsidiary legislation is defined by S.2 of the Interpretation Act 1948 as *"any proclamation, rule, regulation, order, notification, by-law or other instrument made under any Act, Enactment, Ordinance or other lawful authority and having legislative effect."* Parliament enacts the main law and delegates the power to set out the details and technical matters to the respective Ministries. The primary reasons for this may be stated thus. First, Parliament does not have time to set out the details that are required to implement the Act of Parliament. Secondly, the technical aspects are best left to the experts.

The Ministries then would create subsidiary legislation, usually known as Rules or Regulations to implement the main objectives of the parent Act. For example, the Companies Regulations 1966 were created under the Companies Act of 1965 to help implement the basic statutory provisions of the Act such as appointment of auditors, filing of audited accounts and so on.

Subsidiary legislation that contravenes parent legislation or the Federal Constitution is void.

■ Unwritten Law

Unwritten law means the law which is not in the Federal Constitution or made by the Parliament or State Legislative Assembly. There are three types of unwritten law. They are:

- ☐ English common law and rules of equity
- ☐ Judicial decisions/precedents and
- ☐ Customs

☐ English Common Law and Equity

Section 3(1) of the Civil Law Act 1956 provides that English Common Law and Equity will be applicable to the Malaysian legal system, subject to these two restrictions:

1 there should be no local law governing the particular issue; and

2 that part of English law must be suitable to the local customs and circumstances of the people of Malaysia.

This is of course an application of the doctrine of reception discussed above. Rutter (1986) states:

"Reception refers to the process whereby one country (typically a newly-emerging State) voluntarily chooses to accept or receive the law (statute and/or case law) of another country or is involuntarily fused with such laws by an ascendant State."

However, as Section 3(1) clearly states, application of English law is not automatic or unconditional. It will not apply where there is already a local law in existence or where the particular English law is not suitable to local customs and circumstances. Section 3(1)(a) is self-explanatory. In the case of *Attorney-General, Malaysia v Manjeet Singh Dhillon* [1991] 1 M.L.J. 167, the then Supreme Court (the predecessor to the Federal Court) held that in the absence of local law on the issue of contempt of court, the common law on contempt as stated in the English case of *R v Gray* [1900] 2 Q.B. 36 should be applied under Section 3.

English case law has been applied and crystallised in many aspects of Malaysian law, such as commercial, business and company laws. Leading cases from England include *Salomon v Salomon & Co Ltd [1897] AC 22* (company law), *Donoghue v Stevenson* [1932] A.C. 562; 1932 S.C. (H.L.) 31 (law of negligence), *Rowland v Divall* [1923] 2 K.B. 500 (commercial law) are embedded in Malaysian law. Section 3(1)(b) is particularly of interest. Courts have refused to apply English law in many areas such as matters involving family law on the ground that it is unsuitable to the local societal framework with its unique cultural and religious variants.

It is interesting to note however that the courts in Malaysia have refused to apply statutory provisions from England to the Malaysian scenario. Application of Section 3 is therefore limited to case-law. In *Permodalan Plantation Sdn Bhd v Rachuta Sdn Bhd* [1985] 1 M.L.J. 157, the Supreme Court held that a "creature of English statute" did not apply to Malaysia.

☐ Role of case law in development of Malaysian jurisprudence

These are decisions of the courts and are a very important source of law. Case law has contributed to the development of law and the establishment of legal principles. The judges when coming to a decision on a case before them, will do so either by applying an established legal principle or even creating legal principles, as Lord Denning MR frequently did in England. Indeed, decisons of Lord Denning were applied in many cases in Malaysia, one example being the decision in *Western Excavating Ltd v Sharp* (1978) 1 I.C.R. 221 on the issue of constructive dismissal, which was quoted with approval by the then Supreme Court of Malaysia in the case of *Wong Chee Hong v Cathay Organisation (M) Sdn Bhd* (1988) M.L.J .92.

The second manner through which case law contributes to the body of legal principles is when the courts interpret the meaning of particular sections, words or phrases of an Act of Parliament. A case in point is the interpretation of 'workman', as set out in the Industrial Relations Act 1967, which was elaborated and preserved for posterity in the landmark Federal Court decision of *Dr. A. Dutt v Assunta Hospital* (1981) 1 M.L.J. 304. The relevant adage is *certainty through precedent*.

The doctrine of *stare decisis* is firmly entrenched in the Malaysian legal system. In *Public Prosecutor v Datuk Tan Cheng Swee and Anor* [1980] 2 M.L.J .276, 277, Chang Min Tat FCJ said:

> "It is however necessary to reaffirm the doctrine of stare decisis which the Federal Court accepts unreservedly and which it expects the High Court and other inferior courts in a common law system such as ours to follow similarly.....clearly the principle of stare decisis requires more than lip-service."

This doctrine, which is also known as the doctrine of binding judicial precedent, is one where prior decisions of superior courts bind inferior courts in similar situations where the material facts are the same. As explained in Chapter 2, there are two effects of the doctrine of *stare decisis* – the vertical effect and the horizontal effect.

The vertical effect is when the binding effect cascades through the hierarchy of the court structure, namely from the Federal Court down to the magistrates courts and even specialised tribunals such as the Industrial Courts. The application of the doctrine is straightforward in this scenario, as decisions of the superior courts bind the inferior courts. Indeed, the Federal Court has frowned on any attempt by the courts below it to disregard its prior decision: see *Datuk Tan Cheng Swee (supra)* and *Cooperative Central Bank Ltd v Feyen Development Sdn Bhd* [1997] 2 M.L.J. 829 where the Federal Court stated emphatically that the Court of Appeal (and other lower courts) must accept loyally the decisions of the Federal Court.

Horizontal effect of the doctrine applies when courts of the same jurisdiction or at the same level are bound to follow earlier decisions made by their predecessors. This effect normally applies to superior courts. The situation on this issue is rather complex however and there is no hard and fast rule where the Federal Court is concerned. It is not bound by its own previous decisions and is at liberty to depart from its earlier decision should the circumstances demand it. This however is cautiously and sparingly done.

The relevance of the doctrine of *stare decisis* is best summed up by Gopal Sri Ram JCA in the case of *Tunde Apitra and Others v Public Prosecutor* [2001] 1 M.L.J. 259. In rejecting the Prosecution's submission that the Federal Court ought not to follow its own previous decision, the learned judge said this:

"It is bad policy for us as the apex court to leave the law in a state of uncertainty by departing from our own recent decisions. Members of the public must be allowed to arrange their affairs so that they keep well within the framework of the law. They can hardly do this if the judiciary keeps changing its stance upon same issue between brief intervals..."

☐ **Customs**

Customs, or customary law is also a source of law although its impact is not as substantial and as widespread as the other sources. It is peculiar to certain groups of people in certain Malaysian States. The customary law that is applicable to the Malay community is broadly divided into two categories: the *Adat Perpatih* and the *Adat Temenggong*. These basically relate to land, divorce and family matters. It should be noted that the non-Malay communities practised customary law especially in relation to marriage and family matters. However, this was abolished by the *Law Reform (Marriage and Divorce) Act 1976*.

■ **Islamic Law**

Islamic law applies to Muslims only. Family, inheritance and property matters fall within the jurisdiction of the Shari'a courts. The courts are administered by the respective States. *Article 121(1A)* of the Federal Constitution states that the High Court does not have jurisdiction over Shari'a courts.

The Malaysian Judicial System

The Malaysian judicial system is primarily made up of courts which are divided into two – the superior courts and the inferior or the subordinate courts. The powers, jurisdiction and structure of the courts are set out in the Federal Constitution and Acts of Parliament such as the *Courts of Judicature Act 1964* and the *Subordinate Courts Act 1948*. Each court has its own civil and criminal jurisdictions.

The Federal Court, the Court of Appeal and the High Court are considered the superior courts.

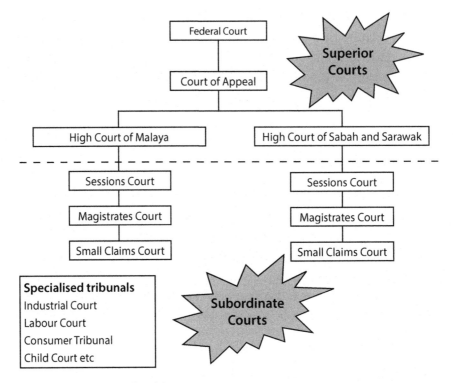

Figure 4.2: The Malaysian Judicial System

■   Superior Courts

☐   Federal Court

The Federal Court is the apex court in Malaysia and is established under Article 121(2) of the Federal Constitution. It is comprised of the Chief Justice of the Federal Court, the President of the Court of Appeal, the Chief Judges of the two High Courts and eight senior judges, called the Federal Court judges. The decisions of the Federal Court bind all the courts below.

There are different aspects to the jurisdiction of the Federal Court – original, appellate, referral and advisory.

☐ **Original jurisdiction,** also known as "exclusive jurisdiction" is invoked by serious legal issues such as the validity of an Act of Parliament and disputes between Federal and State Governments.

☐ **Appellate jurisdiction** empowers the Federal Court to hear appeals of civil decisions of the Court of Appeal where the Federal Court grants leave to do so: *Section 96* of the *Courts of Judicature Act 1964*. Note that leave is not required where criminal appeals are concerned.

☐ **Referral jurisdiction** is triggered when the Court asked to decide on questions of law which are referred by another court.

☐ **Advisory jurisidiction** is when the court is asked to give opinions on matters referred to it by another court or His Majesty Yang Di-Pertuan Agong. See the case of *Government of Malaysia v Government of the State of Kelantan* (1968) 1 M.L.J. 129 where His Majesty Ysng Di-Pertuan Agung referred certain questions on the interpretation of provisions in the Federal Court (Advisory jurisdiction: *Article 130 of the Federal Constitution).*

☐ Court of Appeal

The Court of Appeal was set up under the Constitution (Amendment) Act 1994 and the Courts of Judicature (Amendment) Act 1994 and has appellate jurisdiction only. Unlike the other courts in the court structure, the Court of Appeal does not have original jurisdiction. It hears appeals from the High Court. It was created to serve a second tier appellate court after appeals to the Privy Council in the United Kingdom on civil matters were abolished in 1985. It is the *second highest court* in the hierarchy below the Federal Court.

It hears both civil and criminal appeals. Under sections 67 and 68 of the *Courts of Judicature Act 1964,*the Court is empowered to hear any appeals from the High Court in civil matters where the amount involved is less than RM250,000.00. In cases where the amount is less than that, leave to appeal must be obtained.

There is no limitation on appeals arising from criminal matters. Appeals may be made on questions of law or questions of fact.

The Court of Appeal has the powers to summarily dismiss appeals, confirm, reverse or vary the orders made by the High Court, order a retrial or remit the matter back to the trial court supported by its own opinion.

The court is headed by the President of the Court of Appeal, who is the second most important person in Malaysian judiciary after the Chief Justice.

☐ High Court

There are two High Courts: the High Court in Malaya (based in Kuala Lumpur) and the High Court in Sabah and Sarawak (based in Kuching). These courts go on circuit to other cities. The High Court of Malaya is established under Article 121 (1) of the Federal Constitution. The jurisdiction of the High Court is divided into original, appellate and revisionary. There are two factors which decide on the operation of its jurisdiction – where issues involved are of serious nature or where the subject matter is above RM 250,000.00.

There are four divisions of the High Court: commercial, civil, criminal and special powers and appellate. The High Court has original jurisdiction in the first three divisions.

☐ The **Special Powers and Appellate Division** hears appeals and exercises judicial review over matters from the lower courts and specialised tribunals such as the Industrial Court. It has the powers to hear matters involving the equitable remedies such as injunctions, specific performance and writs of *habeas corpus, mandamus, certiorari* etc.

☐ The **Criminal Division** hear serious criminal cases, especially those which carry the death penalty.

☐ The **Civil Division** primarily deals with divorce and matrimonial causes, bankruptcy and company cases, appointment and control of guardians of infants, disabled persons and their property and grant of probates of wills and letters of administration.

☐ The **Commercial Division** handles commercial cases where the amount involved is more than RM 250,000.00 It hears matters involving companies such as winding up and receivership as well as bankruptcy matters. Much of its powers are regulated by the Rules of the High Court 1980.

■ Subordinate Courts

☐ The Sessions Court

The Sessions Court is the highest in the subordinate court structure. It was established under s. 50 of the *Subordinate Court Act 1948.* It does not serve as an appeal court from the lower courts although it does have supervisory jurisdiction over the magistrates court. Its jurisdiction is determined by both the subject-matter of the case and the amount involved. The Sessions Court has both criminal and civil jurisdiction.

In exercising its criminal jurisdiction, the Court is empowered to try all offences other than offences punishable with death. Where civil jurisdiction is concerned, the Court is empowered to hear accident cases, landlord and tenant, as well as distress and other cases where the amount in dispute does not exceed RM250,000.

☐   **Magistrates Court**

The magistrates court was established by *Section 76* of the *Subordinate Courts Act 1948*. The jurisdiction of the magistates court is set out in *Section 95 as amended by the Subordinate Courts (Amendment) Act 1978*.

Its criminal jurisdiction covers all offences where maximum term of imprisonment does not exceed 10 years and where the offences are punishable with fine only, for example, cheating, robbery, housebreaking, theft. It is empowered to pass any sentence allowed by law not exceeding 5 years imprisonment, a fine up to RM10,000.00, whipping up to 12 strokes; or any combination of the sentence above.

The civil jurisdiction of the magistrates court is limited to cases where the amount in dispute does not exceed RM25,000.

☐   **Small Claims Court**

The jurisdiction is limited to RM5,000 only. There is no need for legal representation in this court and cases are heard by 1st class Magistrates who have legal qualifications.

Exercise 3

John drives home after having a few beers with his friends at a bar. The speed limit is 60 km per hour but John drives at 90 km per hour. As he turns around a curve, he loses control of his car and goes over to the other side of the road, hitting another car that was driving in the opposite direction. James, the driver of the car, is badly injured whereas Jane, his passenger, is killed instantly. Discuss the legal issues arising out of this incident – the types of law that would apply, the courts where the proceedings will commence and the appeal process.

☐   **Specialised Tribunals**

Specialised tribunals are judicial bodies or quasi-judicial bodies that are created to hear and adjudicate on specialised areas. They are creatures of statutes and their jurisdictions are set out in the relevant Act of Parliament. Examples of such tribunals are the Industrial Court (created under the Industrial Relations Act 1967), Labour Court (created under the Employment Act

1955) and the Tribunal for Consumer Claims (created under the Consumer Protection Act 1999). The Industrial Court is a very busy court and issues awards (as its judgments are known) on disputes between employers and workmen (as employees are defined under the IRA). It has its own law report, the Industrial Law Reports.

There is no appeal from judgments of specialised tribunals. Rather, these can be sent to High Court for judicial review. This means that whilst the court will not question the validity of the judgement/award, it will scrutinise the process by which the decision was arrived at and ensure that the process was carried out in accordance with the law.

Exercise 4

The Federal Court in the case of *Wong Chee Hong* v *Cathay Organisation (1988) (supra)* decided that an employee who resigned from his job as a result of his employer's behaviour was forced to do so due to his employer's intention not to proceed with his contract of employment. As such he was constructively dismissed and the court held that the dismissal was without just cause or excuse.

Baloo is the Head of Department of Marketing in Jungle Book Sdn Bhd. The new CEO, Shere Khan, informs Baloo that he is reassigned to head the Marketing Unit, which is part of the Department Baloo heads. Shere Khan informs Baloo that this is in line with the company policy that top management executives should "go back to the grass root level to reacquaint themselves with junior staff". Baloo does not accept Shere Khan's reasons and believes that Shere Khan is trying to force him resign from his employment. This belief is strengthened by the fact that Mowgli, Baloo's assistant is promoted as the Head of Department and Baloo is now directly reporting to Mowgli. Unhappy at the turn of events, Baloo resigns and files a complaint of wrongful dismissal against Jungle Book Sdn Bhd.

The Industrial Court, following the decision of the Federal Court in *Wong Chee Hong* rules that Baloo was constructively dismissed and orders Jungle Book Sdn Bhd to pay him damages. The employer files the case in the High Court for judicial review. The High Court judge refuses to follow the Federal Court, stating that (a) the facts in Baloo's case are different from *Wong Chee Hong* (they are not) and (b) constructive dismissal is unique to the English legal system and is not suitable to the local norms and customs of Malaysia.

Baloo now seeks your advice. Is the High Court correct? What would you suggest Baloo's next course of action be?

Conclusion

This chapter demonstrates the practicalities of the law in the Malaysian context – how law is created and where it is applied. It is a living thing that has developed through centuries and continues to develop. In the same manner as Chapters 2 and 3, this chapter explored the constitution of Malaysia, the formal sources of law, and the court structures. Knowledge of the law is crucial and as the famous adage goes: *Ignorantia juris non excusat* (Ignorance of the law is not an excuse).

Key concepts

1   Federal Constitution is the supreme law of the land.

2   Legislation is a significant source of law in the Malaysian legal system. Reference should always be made to statutes first.

3   Case law is the second significant source of law. The legal principles derived from judgments of cases form the body of laws which are considered as legal authorities.

4   The hierarchy of courts is an important factor in establishing the legal principles stated above. Judicial precedent or the doctrine of *stare decisis* is entrenched in the Malaysian legal system.

4

Further reading

Hamzah, W., (2012) *A First Look at the Malaysian Legal System* (2009) Malaysia: Oxford Fajar Sdn Bhd.

Lee, M. P and Detta I. J., (2014) *Business Law* 2nd ed Oxford: Oxford University Press.

Noordin, S.M., and Supramaniam, S., (2013) Update: an Overview of Malaysian legal System and Research. Available at http://www.nyulawglobal.org/globalex/Malaysia1.html#OriginsofModernMalaysianLaw [Accessed 22 May 2016]

Official website of the Attorney-General's Chambers : http://www.agc.gov.my [Accessed 22 May 2016]

Official website of the Ministry of Justice: http://www.kehakiman.gov.my

Rheinstein, M., (1956) Types of Reception. In *The Anthology of Swiss Culture*. Available at: http://www.legalanthology.ch/globalization/3-contributions/types-of-reception [Accessed 22 May 2016].

Rutter, M.,(1986) *The Applicable Law in Singapore and Malaysia* MLJ 415.

Wu, M.A., *The Malaysian Legal System* (3rd Ed) 2007 Malaysia: Pearson Sdn Bhd.

Abbreviations

M.L.J: Malayan Law Journal

5 The Law of Obligations

Yvonne McLaren

On a day to day basis we are likely to engage in a variety of contractual situations whether we are aware of it or not. Think of a regular routine of stopping at the coffee shop to buy our coffee and cake for our daily treat. In a legal sense this might be defined as a consumer contract with all the corresponding rights and obligations, i.e. our right to have the products as requested, free from defect or issue, and the obligation of the seller to provide our requests. Further we have an obligation to pay for the products and the seller has a right to receive remuneration for the product given. Effectively this example provides us with an introduction to the law of contract.

In the next six chapters, we will be exploring the law of obligations. As will be seen, these range from voluntary obligations we choose to enter, to obligations we owe to our fellow citizens whether we like it or not (involuntary obligations). This chapter starts with an overview of legal obligations in general and then introduces the law of contract.

What is a legal obligation?

Effectively we can say that there is a distinction between: a legal 'duty' – owed to everybody and a legal 'obligation' – owed to a specific person. So for example, you owe a duty to take reasonable care not to injure people. If you do injure someone, you may have an obligation to compensate him or her. Historically, the Scots law of obligations came from principles of Roman law, although the increased influence of English law since the 18th century means that the law in the two countries is now very similar, but please note, not identical.

During the study of contract law, the emphasis for students is to provide authority for conclusions and assertions made. The main principles of the law of obligations have been set down and developed by judicial decisions (common law), rather than enacted by Parliament (statute law or legislation).

Categories of obligations

■ Obligations voluntarily undertaken

Obligations may be undertaken by one person (unilateral voluntary obligations) or be undertaken by more than one party by agreement. These we may define as contracts.

■ Obligations imposed by law

The law imposes some obligations on us whether we want to be bound by them or not. This includes situations where someone has benefited at someone else's expense (unjustified enrichment) and where someone has caused damage or injury to another person (delict/tort), which will be further explored in Chapters 8-10 of this book.

■ Voluntary obligations: unilateral and bilateral, gratuitous and onerous

Unilateral gratuitous obligations and gratuitous promises

From the introductory example we saw a situation where both parties had obligations placed upon them, and generally we can say that for every right there is a corresponding obligation and for every obligation there is a right. With a gratuitous obligation only one party is legally bound. Please note that this situation is not generally regarded as enforceable in England because of the doctrine of consideration (unless written within a deed). However they may be enforceable in Scotland if certain conditions are fulfilled:

Genuine promise

It is important that the promise is genuine and is not merely expression of intention or expectation by the party. This is best seen in the following case example.

Gray v Johnson **1928 S.C. 569**

Facts of the case:

Gray claimed that Johnston had proposed to him that, if he went to live with Johnston and looked after him, he would make Gray his heir. Gray did so but Johnston died without leaving Gray his property.

Court decision:

The court dismissed Gray's claim, saying that what Johnston had said was nothing more than an expression of intention. There was no enforceable promise.

In Scotland, a promise may be binding on the promisor and does not need to be accepted by the other party in order to be binding. It must be communicated to the other person before he can rely on it.

It must be possible to prove the existence of the promise in the required way. Under s.1(2)(a)(ii) of the Requirements of Writing (Scotland) Act 1995, writing is required for the constitution of a gratuitous unilateral obligation, except an obligation undertaken in the course of business. Here we see the Scots law dynamic at play, where the obligation is prima facie assumed to exist if it is an obligation undertaken in the course of business. Previously, gratuitous obligations could only be proved by 'writ or oath.' The common law position was established via this next case.

Smith v Oliver **1911 S.C. 103**

Facts of the case:

Trustees for a church brought an action against the executors of Mrs. Oliver for payment of the cost of structural alterations to the church. They claimed that Mrs. Oliver had urged them to have the work done and had promised to leave a bequest in her will to pay for it, but she had failed to do so.

Court decision:

The promise of the bequest could only be proved by Mrs. Oliver's writ. Lord President Dunedin said: "There is in truth no contract at all averred here, merely a promise to pay. And if that is so, I suppose that it is well settled law that a gratuitous promise to pay can be proved only by writ."

■   Voluntary obligations: essential elements of a contract

In most voluntary obligations, both parties owe obligations to each other: for example, I agree to sell you my car. In this example, I must deliver the car to you and you must pay the price.

Effectively we can say that there are five essential elements of a contract:

1 **Intention to be legally bound.** Here the parties must appear to have intended to enter a legally binding agreement.

2 *Consensus in idem.* This Latin maxim can be translated simply as 'a meeting of minds' indicating that the parties must have agreement on the same thing.

3 **Capacity.** This reflects the need of the parties to an agreement, to have the requisite legal capacity to enter into a contract.

4 **Formality.** This reflects the situation where the law sometimes imposes formalities on the formation of a contract, and these must be complied with.

5 **Legality.** It is understandable that those agreements which may be deemed as illegal agreements will be treated as void. This will be expanded on later but effectively we can say that the agreement has no legal effect.

Let's expand and consider these elements more fully below:

1. Intention to be legally bound

There will only be a valid contract if the parties intended to enter into a legally binding agreement. There are situations however where the law presumes there is no intention to be legally bound. Some examples of this may be found within the following kinds of agreements:

(a) **Social agreements:** for example, an arrangement to meet someone: here it is presumed not to be intended to be legally binding unless there is strong evidence to the contrary.

(b) **Domestic agreements**: for example, an agreement to pay a spouse or child a periodic allowance. Traditionally this was presumed not to be legally binding unless there was evidence to the contrary.

(c) **Agreements not involving patrimonial interests**: a patrimonial interest may be defined as something of value which the individual stands to lose if the agreement is not enforced. Please note that agreements without patrimonial interest are presumed not intended to be legally binding unless there is strong evidence to the contrary.

(d) **Collective bargaining agreements**: collective agreements between trade unions and employers were presumed at common law not to be intended to have legal effect. Note however that under s.179 of the Trade Union and Labour Relations (Consolidation) Act 1992, such agreements are deemed not to be intended to be legally enforceable unless put into writing which states that the agreement is to have legal effect.

(e) **Commercial agreements**: the law presumes that parties to commercial contracts do intend to be legally bound, unless there is clear and unambiguous evidence that this is not the case.

2. *Consensus in idem*

We started off our discussion of contract by introducing the notion of obligations and noted that obligations may be voluntary by agreement or involuntary (imposed by law). The voluntary nature of contracts suggests that we have discretion and choice over what we agree to do, in other words we consent to the terms and conditions and obligations we may be required to undertake.

Where the parties do in fact have the intention to be legally bound we may observe the process as follows:

Offer

Here the offer is a statement or course of action which clearly indicates that the person making it is willing to be legally bound to its terms. Note that an offer has no effect until communicated to the offeree.

It is very important that we are able to determine that we have a distinct and definite offer and to distinguish this from a willingness to negotiate. The law distinguishes between an offer and an invitation to treat, which is an invitation for others to make offers. Most advertisements, shop displays and catalogues are invitations to treat. This can be seen, for example, in the following case.

Pharmaceutical Society of Great Britain v Boots Cash Chemists (Southern) Ltd **[1953] 1 All E.R. 482**

Facts of the case:

The defendant's branch at Edgeware, London was adapted to a self-service system whereby customers selected goods from the shelves and took them to a cash desk to pay the price.

One section of the shelves was set out with drugs included in the poisons list referred to in s.17 of the Pharmacy and Poisons Act 1933, though they were not dangerous drugs and did not require a doctor's prescription. Section 18 of that Act required the sale of such drugs to take place in the presence of a pharmacist. All sales of drugs on the poisons list were supervised at the cash desk by a pharmacist.

The Society, which had a duty to enforce the Act, brought an action against Boots on the basis that the display of the drugs constituted an offer, which the customer accepted when he selected goods from the shelves. The sale was thus completed without supervision.

Court decision:

The display of drugs on the shelves was not an offer but an invitation to treat. The contract was made when the assistant at the cash desk accepted the customer's offer to buy what had been chosen. The presence of the pharmacist at the cash desk fulfilled the requirements for supervision under the Act.

Please note that a reply to a request for information is not usually regarded as an offer to deal on those terms.

General and specific offers

Bearing in mind the obligations that may result, it is important to further define the difference between general and specific offers.

An offer can be made to a specific person or to the world at large. See for example this classic case.

> ### Carlill v Carbolic Smokeball Co [1893] 1 Q.B. 256
>
> **Facts of the case:**
>
> The defendants were proprietors of a medical preparation called 'The Carbolic Smoke Ball.' They advertised in a number of newspapers that they would pay £100 to anyone who contracted influenza after using the ball three times a day for two weeks. Mrs. Carlill used the ball as advertised and caught flu. She sued for the £100 promised by the advertisement. Various defences were raised; in particular it was claimed that the advertisement was not intended to constitute an offer, since it would amount to an attempt to contract with the whole world, which was impossible.
>
> **Court decision:**
>
> There was a binding contract. The advertisement was an offer to the whole world, which was accepted by those who fulfilled the conditions. Mrs. Carlill had fulfilled the conditions, and was thus entitled to be paid the £100.

An offer does not remain open for acceptance forever. An offer may lapse through:

(I) **Rejection**: an offer lapses when rejected and person rejecting it cannot then change his mind and accept.

(ii) **Lapse of time**: an offer expressed to be open for a specific period of time lapses on expiry of the time. Please note that any other offer lapses after a reasonable time.

(iii) **Death**: an offer lapses if the offeror dies before it is accepted.

(iv) **Mental incapacity**: an offer lapses if the offeror becomes insane after making it but before it is accepted.

(v) **Revocation**: an offer can usually be revoked or withdrawn at any time before acceptance. Revocation is not effective until notified to the offeree.

Acceptance

An unconditional offer must be followed by unconditional acceptance where there must be consensus on the fundamental or material issues. Requirements for valid acceptance include the following:

(a) **Acceptance must match offer**, i.e. acceptance must match the offer in all material terms. In other words it must not introduce new conditions or qualifications, or it is regarded as a counter-offer. A counter-offer effectively acts as a rejection of the original offer, so that original offer lapses and is no longer open for acceptance.

Note for example the issue of standard forms. Most businesses use their own standard forms so there may be no contract if B's standard form acceptance does not match A's standard form offer.

(b) **Acceptance must be communicated**. The general rule is that acceptance is of no effect until communicated to the offeror.

(I) *Postal rule* – where an acceptance has been sent through the post, it becomes effective from the time it is posted, not from the time it is received. See for example this case.

Jacobsen Sons & Co v Underwood & Son Ltd **(1894) 21 R. 654**

Facts of the case:

On March 2 Underwood offered to buy straw from Jacobsen, the offer stating that it was to remain open until 6 March. On 6 March, Jacobsen wrote and posted an acceptance of the offer, but this was not delivered to Underwood until March 7. Underwood claimed there was no contract because the acceptance had not reached them until after the stated date and they refused to accept the straw when Jacobsen tried to deliver it.

Court decision:

Because the acceptance was concluded at the time it was posted, the offer had been accepted in time and there was a contract.

Note: this rule does not apply to other forms of communication of acceptances, (this will be discussed further when we consider electronic contracts) in Chapter 6.

(ii) *Implied Acceptance* – acceptance of an offer may be implied by the conduct of the parties, without any written or oral communication of acceptance. It is not generally possible to impose acceptance by silence.

(c) **Acceptance must be timeous**. In other word an offer must be accepted within the prescribed time, or a reasonable time.

3. Capacity

As previously stated above, parties to the contract must have the requisite legal capacity to enter into a contract. Please note that there are limits on the contractual capacity of some categories of people.

Young people

The law is found in the Age of Legal Capacity (Scotland) Act 1991. This replaced centuries of division when young people under the age of majority used to be categorized into pupils and minors. These concepts disappeared and a new single tier system took its place. Effectively this act provides that persons under the age of 16 have no capacity to enter into contracts or other transactions having legal effect. Any obligations must be undertaken on their behalf by their guardians. Any obligation undertaken by a person under 16 is regarded as void, except:

(a) Child aged 12 or over can make a will or consent to adoption.

(b) Child of any age can consent to medical treatment if capable of understanding the consequences of the treatment.

(c) Child of any age can enter into a transaction of a kind commonly entered into by someone of his age and circumstances, provided the terms are not unreasonable.

Persons aged 16 and 17 have full contractual capacity, but can apply to the court to have prejudicial contracts set aside. A person has until his 21st birthday to challenge a prejudicial transaction made when he was 16 or 17. Note that a prejudicial transaction is one which a reasonably prudent adult would not have entered into and which is likely to cause substantial prejudice to the young person. The following transactions cannot be challenged:

□ A will.

□ Consent to medical treatment or adoption.

□ Steps taken in legal proceedings.

□ Transactions entered in the course of the young person's trade, business or profession.

□ Transactions where the young person fraudulently misrepresented his age or other material fact.

□ Transactions the young person ratified after reaching 18 in the knowledge of the right to challenge.

□ Transactions ratified by the court under s.4 of the Act.

Exercise

In a desire to get fit, Bob, aged 17, signed a yearly gym membership contract. However, six months later, Bob is finding the monthly payments a struggle. He would like to get out of this contract, but the gym is holding him to the full year's membership. Advise Bob on his legal position.

Persons of unsound mind

Traditionally 'insane persons' an old-fashioned expression used in the old case law, have been held to have no contractual capacity and any purported transaction will be void. Where a guardian has been appointed, lack of mental capacity is regarded as proved even if person was lucid when entering the contract. Where no guardian has been appointed, it must be proved that person lacked mental capacity at the time the contract was entered into.

Loudon v Elder's Curator Bonis **1923 S.L.T. 226 (OH)**

Facts of the case:

Elder, a Dundee merchant, ordered goods from Loudon on March 23 and 28. On March 31, before any of the goods were delivered, Elder was certified insane and on April 1 Loudon was informed that the contracts were cancelled. Loudon sued Elder's *curator bonis* (the former term for what is now called a guardian) for damages for breach of contract. Elder was proved to have lacked mental capacity at the time the orders were given.

Court decision:

There was no liability for breach of contract as the orders were null and void.

Intoxicated persons

If person was incapable through drink or drugs any contract will be void but the person must be truly incapable of understanding. Generally the courts will not reduce these contracts. See for example the following case.

Taylor v Provan **(1864) 2M. 1226**

Facts of the case:

Provan went to Taylor's farm and offered to buy 31 cattle at £14 per head, but Taylor refused to accept less than £15. After trying unsuccessfully to purchase cattle elsewhere, Provan returned to Taylor's farm the worse for drink and offered £15 per head, which was accepted by Taylor. Taylor later brought an action against Provan for the price of the cattle, and Provan claimed that he had been incapable, through intoxication, of entering into the contract.

Court decision:

The contract must be repudiated as soon as person regains his senses. Provan was not so intoxicated as not to know what he was doing, and so was bound by the contract.

5

Enemy aliens

These are persons voluntarily living or carrying on business in an enemy country in wartime. An enemy alien has no contractual capacity in the UK.

4. Formalities required for valid contracts

The general rule is that there are no special formalities required to make a contract in Scotland. Most contracts will be equally valid whether entered into in writing, orally, or inferred from the conduct of the parties. In disputes about whether a contract has been formed, both written and oral evidence can be heard. However; we must observe the formalities demanded of the Requirements of Writing (Scotland) Act 1995. This act requires a written document for the formation of:

(a) **Contracts involving an interest in land**, i.e. any contract or unilateral obligation for the creation, transfer, variation or extinction of an interest in land must be in writing – includes leases for more than one year and security rights, such as mortgages.

(b) **Unilateral gratuitous obligations**. As previously stated these must be constituted in writing unless undertaken in the course of a business.

(c) **Trusts**. These must be formed in writing if a person wants to make himself sole trustee of his own property.

(d) **Wills** or any other testamentary dispositions must be in writing.

Note: a probative document is one which proves itself authentic in court without need for further evidence. A document will be probative if the signature of the parties is witnessed by one person who signs as witness, and whose name and address are included in the document.

Note that a contract not properly embodied in writing may be made enforceable by the subsequent actions of the parties. Under the Requirements of Writing (Scotland) Act 1995, this arises where one of the parties to the contract has:

(i) Acted in reliance on the contract; and

(ii) Done this with the knowledge and acquiescence of the other party; and

(iii) Would be adversely affected to a material extent if the other party was allowed to withdraw from the contract.

The Legal Writing (Counterparts and Delivery) (Scotland) Act 2015 now allows for a written contract to be made by two or more parties each signing separate copies of an identical document. It also provides for delivery of traditional contractual documents by electronic means agreed between the parties, or if no means is agreed, by whatever means is reasonable in the circumstances. These provisions help to modernize the making of contracts in Scots law, where electronic documents are fast becoming the norm.

There will be further discussion of electronic contracts in the next chapter.

5. Legality

(a) **Contracts may be illegal** either under common law or statute.

Contracts which may be deemed illegal at common law include a contract to commit a crime or delict, a contract with an enemy alien in wartime, a contract to defraud the revenue, a contract involving corruption in public life, a contract detrimental to administration of justice. Please note that if a contract is illegal from the start, it is totally void, ie. a nullity.

Contracts which may be illegal under statute depend on the wording of the statute. An Act may provide that a contract is 'void', 'unlawful' or 'unenforceable'. Further, the statute may provide for a criminal sanction without making a contract void.

(b) **Contracts contrary to public policy.**

Contracts regarded as contrary to public policy are void. The concept of public policy is subject to change. Examples of contracts contrary to public policy are:

(i) Contracts in restraint of personal liberty.

(ii) Contracts prejudicial to freedom of marriage.

(iii) Contracts furthering sexual immorality.

(c) **Contracts deemed unenforceable**

Main categories:

(i) *Gambling agreements*

"The court does not exist for settling disputes as to who had the winning number in a lottery." Per Lord Young in *Christison v McBride* (1881) 9R. 34.

These are agreements which people will generally enter into by way of placing a 'bet' on a variety of sporting events or other activities, e.g. who will be this year's winner at the Grand National horse race. It has been said that the UK is hypocritical in its treatment of gambling activities, as it on the one hand will impose a tax on those who place bets, but on the other both Scots and English Courts have been reluctant to act as judges with regard to any disputes which arise out of the same agreements, and regarded them as *sponsiones ludicrae* (games of chance), and not matters that could be decided in court. Some have said that the courts regarded such agreements as simply below their dignity and not worth the waste of valuable time. Historically it may be reflective of the impact of the Church in everyday matters including law.

The current position is established via the Gambling Act 2005. As a result of section 335 of the 2005 Act, the doctrine of *sponsiones ludicrae* in relation to gambling contracts has now been repealed. It states that: "the fact that a contract relates to gambling shall not prevent its enforcement."

The significance of this act is that it means that the Scottish courts now have to deal with disputes between parties to a gambling agreement and will be required to provide them with a remedy, which was not previously the case. The following cases are based on the pre-existing common law.

Robertson v Balfour **1938 S.C. 207**

Facts of the case:

Robertson had entered into gambling agreements with Balfour, a bookmaker, to place bets on two horses (Swift & True and Scotch Horse). Both horses won their respective races but Robertson received a mere £10 in winnings from Balfour. In fact Balfour owed Robertson another £33 in winnings. Robertson agreed that he would give Balfour extra time to pay him the balance.

Court decision:

Robertson could not enforce the agreement against Balfour to pay out the additional £33. This was a gambling debt and the courts would not enforce such an agreement.

Ferguson v Littlewoods Pools Ltd **1997 S.L.T. 309**

Facts of the case:

The members of a pools syndicate had won several million pounds via a football coupon. They were unaware that the agent for Littlewoods Pools had not forwarded the stake money. When the theft was discovered, the members demanded that Littlewoods should honour the winning ticket.

Court decision:

Lord Coulsfield (Outer House, Court of Session) held that the contract between the syndicate and Littlewoods was an example of a gambling or gaming contract and it was therefore unenforceable. Lord Coulsfield refused to order Littlewoods to pay out the sum owed to the syndicate.

Please note that the 2005 Act now gives more protection for members of gambling syndicates.

> **Robertson v Anderson 2003 S.L.T. 235**
>
> **Facts of the case:**
>
> Two female friends regularly attended Bingo sessions together. On one occasion they attended the Mecca Bingo Hall in Drumchapel from their homes in Dunoon. Anderson won 3 prizes £390, £8000 and £100,000. Robertson claimed that she was owed half of the National Prize of £100,000 – a claim that Anderson dismissed. Evidence was heard which established that Robertson and Anderson had an agreement that they would share equally any money that they might win during a game of Bingo.
>
> This case was heard prior to the 2005 Act and an action would have been rejected so the question was about whether the agreement between Robertson and Anderson was a collateral contract and therefore, enforceable, despite the fact that it was slightly tainted by association with the main gambling contract between Anderson and Mecca.
>
> **Court decision:**
>
> The Inner House held that Robertson could enforce the collateral contract that she had with Anderson. Collateral contracts are linked to another contract and they often give rise to a completely separate set of rights and duties. Their contract related to gaming but it was not itself a gaming contract. The crucial difference between this case and Ferguson was whether Anderson was under an obligation to share with Robertson the winnings which she received, rather than the enforcement of a gaming contract.

5

(ii) *Contracts in restraint of trade also known as restrictive covenants*

We can define restrictive covenants as contracts or terms in contracts which restrict a person's right to trade or carry on a profession. They may be used in employment contracts, contracts for sale of a business or *solus* agreements.

Please note that restrictive covenants are unenforceable unless the restriction is fair and reasonable in the circumstances. In order to determine whether the restrictive covenant may be considered fair and reasonable the court will examine the following:

(I) *The interests to be protected*, i.e. the person seeking to impose the restriction must have legitimate interests to protect, such as trade secrets.

Bluebell Apparel Ltd v Dickinson **1978 S.C. 16**

Facts of the case:

Bluebell manufactured Wrangler jeans, selling them in around 120 countries. Dickinson trained with Bluebell and became a manager at one of their factories. While there he acquired knowledge of Bluebell's methods which were unknown to their competitors. Dickinson's contract of employment contained conditions which stated that he would not disclose or use any of Bluebell's trade secrets, and that he would not enter into employment with any competitor of Bluebell for a period of two years after the end of his employment. Six months after joining Bluebell, Dickinson left the company to take up employment with a manufacturer of Levi jeans.

Court decision:

The restriction was reasonable in its scope and, as Bluebell had a legitimate interest in protecting its trade secrets, the restriction would be enforced.

(ii) *The extent of the restriction*

The restriction must not be for a longer time or cover a greater geographical area than is needed to reasonably protect the interests of the party imposing the restriction.

Dumbarton Steamboat Co Ltd v Macfarlane **(1899) 1 F. 993**

Facts of the case:

MacFarlane was a partner in a firm of carriers which was sold to Dumbarton Steamboat Co. The partners, including Macfarlane, were to be employed by the company and undertook (a) to try to obtain customers for the company and, (b) not to carry on or be concerned with any competing business in the UK for ten years. Three years later MacFarlane, who had been dismissed from the company, began business on his own account in Dumbarton.

Court decision:

The defender could be interdicted from canvassing the customers of the former firm, but the restriction against carrying on business anywhere in the UK was unreasonable and therefore unenforceable, and the court would not rewrite the clause to confine it to a reasonable area.

Nordenfelt v Maxim Nordenfelt Guns and Ammunition Co **[1894] A.C. 535**

Facts of the case:

Nordenfelt sold his guns and ammunition business to a company which he set up. He agreed in writing that he would not compete with the Nordenfelt Company. Under the agreement, he received £237,000 in cash, £50,000 in shares and remained managing director of the company for 7 years at a salary of £2,000 per year and a share of the profits. Two years later, the company combined with the Maxim Gun and Ammunition Company.

Nordenfelt entered into a new covenant which provided he would not engage in the business of manufacturing guns, or in any business competing with the company, anywhere in the world for 25 years with another arms manufacturer. Nordenfelt then breached this restriction and the company sought an injunction to prevent him doing so.

Court decision:

Although the restriction was unusually wide, the nature of the business and the limited number of customers (government agencies), meant that it was necessary for the protection of the company's goodwill. Nordenfelt had received a considerable sum for the business and there were no public policy reasons for refusing to uphold the restriction.

5

(iii) *The public interest*

Courts have discretion to refuse to enforce a restriction which is contrary to the public interest.

It has been suggested that restrictive covenants are more likely to be enforced in cases involving the sale of a business than they are in employment contracts, as they are unwilling to restrict an employee's ability to earn a living. An unreasonable restriction will be completely unenforceable - the court will not rewrite the clause to make it reasonable. See for example Dumbarton Steamboat Co Ltd v Macfarlane as before.   If it is possible to sever the unreasonable restrictions from the reasonable ones, the court will enforce the reasonable restrictions.

Mulvein v Murray **1908 S.C. 528**

Facts of the case:

Mulvein, a boot and shoe seller, hired Murray as a salesman under an agreement by which Murray was bound not to sell to or canvass any of Mulvein's customers or to sell or travel in any of the areas traded in by Mulvein for twelve months after his employment was terminated. Murray left his employment with Mulvein and took up a job as a salesman for a boot and shoe manufacturer in Ayr. Mulvein brought an action for interdict.

Court decision:

The restriction on selling to or canvassing Mulvein's customers was reasonable and valid. The other part of the clause was too wide and invalid, but as the agreement was severable, the courts would enforce the reasonable restriction.

Conclusion

In a twenty-four hour, global market it is important to understand that in addition to the advantages of being able to interact within this global environment, we must observe the rights and obligations to which we have agreed. Our starting point may generally be viewed as common law, where cases that have been heard by our courts have moved the direction of our rights and obligations forward. As the market has expanded, Scotland has looked towards subsequent legislation to provide the appropriate legal infrastructure to protect the parties to these complex global exchanges.

Further reading

Ashton, C, et al. (2012) *Understanding Scots Law* 2nd edition Edinburgh: W. Green. Chapter 7 pp.240-255.

Black, G., (ed) (2015) *Business Law in Scotland* 3rd edition Edinburgh: W. Green. Chapter 4, pp.114-134.

Black, G., (2014) *Woolman on Contract* 5th Edition Edinburgh: W. Green.

MacNeill, I.,(ed) (2014) *Scots Commercial Law*. Edinburgh: Avizandum Publishing Ltd.

MacQueen, H., and Thomson, J., (2012) *Contract Law in Scotland* 3rd Edition Haywards Heath: Bloomsbury Professional.

6 Contract Law – Some Specific Issues

Yvonne McLaren

We have seen in the previous chapter how parties seek to determine obligations via their voluntary agreements. There are, however, situations which may become problematic for the parties and will directly affect the validity of some contracts. The chapter also discusses the important topic of contractual terms, and the law relating to making contracts by electronic means, an area of growing importance.

Validity of contracts

■ Void, voidable and unenforceable contracts

1 **Void contract**. Effectively these may be regarded as having been a nullity from the start. The effect of this results in the agreement having no legal effect. Significantly for third parties this also means that no rights can be transferred by a void contract.

2 **Voidable contract**. These may be agreements which either one or both parties are entitled to have set aside. Please note however that the contract is valid and continues to be effective until this is done. Rights and obligations can be transferred under the contract before it is set aside.

3 **Unenforceable contract**. As stated before, there may be circumstances in which contracts are legal and possible to perform, but which the courts will not allow for policy reasons.

■   Agreement improperly obtained

As discussed in Chapter 5, fundamental to the agreement is *consensus in idem*. In other words both parties must consent to the material terms of a contract. If however the consent of one of the parties has not been properly obtained, the contract may be void or voidable.

There are a variety of situations in which a court may find that the agreement has been improperly obtained. For example:

Facility and circumvention

When we consider this scenario we must understand the terms being used. *Facility* can be considered in terms of mental weakness, i.e. an individual may suffer from mental weakness making them vulnerable in their ability to provide consensus. *Circumvention* on the other hand can be seen as an action or set of circumstances which effectively allow one of the parties to persuade someone to act against their intentions or interests.

We can suggest that the contract may be voidable if one party can prove that when he consented to the agreement:

1 he was in a state of facility,

2 the other party took advantage of this to induce him to enter the contract and

3 he suffered some loss because of the contract.

Anderson v The Beacon Fellowship **1992 S.L.T. 111**

Facts of the case:

The Fellowship, a religious association, rented a hall from Anderson and in 1985 entered into missives to purchase it. Representatives of the organisation visited Anderson and allegedly pressed their religious practice upon him. Anderson gave a number of donations to the association and he now sought to have them repaid, on the basis that they had been obtained by fraud and circumvention while he was in a weak and facile condition. He claimed that, at the time, he had been suffering from serious illness and depression, and that the fellowship had put considerable pressure on him.

Court decision:

This pressure was sufficient to amount to circumvention and, if proved, would invalidate the transaction.

McGilvary v Gilmartin **1986 S.L.T. 89**

Facts of the case:

The pursuer disponed to the defender, her daughter, a house which she, the pursuer, had inherited from her own father and which she had always intended to give to her son. Mrs. McGilvary averred that in 1980, her daughter had come to stay with her and her husband, who died shortly afterwards. The death left Mrs. McGilvary in a weak physical and mental state. She claimed that, while she was in this condition, her daughter took her to a solicitor's office and persuaded her to sign over the property.

Court decision:

This was sufficient to amount to circumvention. There was no need to prove actual fraud.

Undue influence

This may arise where parties to contract are in a relationship where one naturally has trust and confidence in the other and the stronger party takes unfair advantage of this to obtain an agreement detrimental to the weaker party. Examples of this may found within parent/child, doctor/patient, and solicitor/client relationships. A contract is voidable where undue influence is proved.

Gray v Binny **(1879) 7 R. 332**

Facts of the case:

Gray, who was aged 24 and heir under a deed of entail, executed a deed by which he parted with his rights in an estate for very much less than the true value. He was persuaded to enter the agreement by his mother and her legal advisor Binny, to whom she was deeply in debt. The mother died soon afterwards and Gray brought an action for reduction.

Court decision:

The court reduced the agreement on the basis that Gray had been unduly influenced by his mother. "It seems to me to be very clear that a deed so prejudicial to the granter, and obtained in such circumstances, cannot, when challenged, be allowed to stand". (Lord Shand).

6

Force and fear

A contract may be held as void if one party can show he was induced to consent to it by force or threats of force; or because he was afraid of the consequences of not consenting. Force or threat must be such as would overcome the will of a reasonable person and must be legitimate.

Earl of Orkney v Vinfra **(1606) Mor.16,481**

Facts of the case:

The Earl brought a claim against Vinfra for payment of 2,000 merks on the basis of a written contract signed by Vinfra. Vinfra contended that the contract was null and void because his signature had been induced by force and fear. He claimed that he had been summoned to the Earl's castle and that the Earl had ordered him to sign the contract, which had already been signed by the Earl. Vinfra refused, whereupon the Earl drew his sword and threatened to kill Vinfra if he did not sign.

Court decision:

The contract was void having been induced by fear of force.

Error

Effectively error may make a contract voidable or void. The outcome depends on the kind of error and how it is made. Some distinctions:

- ☐ **Error in fact**: This may be defined as an error about some fact pertaining to the contract, such as the subject matter or the price. An error in fact may affect the validity of the contract.

- ☐ **Error in law**: This may be defined as an error as to how the contract is affected by the general law. Usually, error in law does not affect the validity of the contract.

- ☐ **Collateral error:** This may be defined as an error as to some minor part of the contract which does not affect the substance of it.

- ☐ **Essential error:** This may be defined as an error affecting the substantials of the contract. It is usually said that only essential error can invalidate a contract. Five kinds of error have been identified as potentially essential: these include error as to the nature of the contract, error as to the identity of the other party (only where this is material to the contract), error as to the subject matter of the contract, error as to price and finally error as to quality, quantity or extent.

Categories of Error:

(i) **Common error**: where both parties have made the same mistake. Common error does not normally invalidate a contract.

Dawson v Muir **(1851) 13 D. 843**

Facts of case:

Dawson entered into a contract to buy from Muir some vats which were sunk into the ground. Both parties thought the vats were empty and Dawson paid around £2 for them. In fact, the vats were later discovered to contain white lead which was worth around £300. The seller tried to have the contract reduced on the grounds of error.

Court decision:

This was common error and the contract was valid.

(ii) **Mutual error**: where parties are at cross-purposes, each thinking a different thing has been agreed.

Please note that the effects of mutual error vary. If one party's interpretation is more reasonable, court may enforce the contract in his favour:

6

Muirhead & Turnbull v Dickson **(1905) 13 S.L.T. 151**

Facts of the case:

Muirhead & Turnbull supplied a piano to Dickson at a price of £26 to be paid at 15s per month. Dickson fell behind with the payments and the pursuers wished to take back the piano. They did so on the basis that either there was no contract between the parties, because there was no consensus, or that the contract was one of hire purchase, so that in either case the ownership of the piano remained with Muirhead & Turnbull. Dickson claimed that the contract was one of sale by instalments, so that ownership of the piano had passed to Dickson.

Court decision:

Muirhead and Turnbull had intended to make a contract of hire-purchase and Dickson had intended to make a contract of purchase paid by instalments, but on the evidence Dickson was justified in his understanding of the contract. The pursuer's action for redelivery of the piano failed, the correct remedy being for the unpaid instalments.

If there is no preferred interpretation, the court will hold that there is no contract:

Raffles v Wichelhaus **(1864) 2 Hurl. & C. 906**

Facts of the case:

The defendant in this English case agreed to buy cotton from the plaintiff, the contract providing that it was to arrive 'ex Peerless'. In fact, there were two ships of that name, both sailing from Mumbai with a cargo of cotton, one sailing in October and one in December. The buyer thought his cotton was to be shipped in October, but the seller intended to ship the cotton on the Peerless sailing in December.

Court decision:

There was no contract because there was no *consensus in idem*. This was mutual error and the court could find no reason for preferring one party's interpretation to the others.

(iii) **Uninduced unilateral error**: this arises where only one party has made a mistake and the other has done nothing to induce his error. This will not generally invalidate a contract.

Royal Bank of Scotland v Purvis **1990 S.L.T. 262**

Facts of the case:

The bank sued the defender as guarantor of her husband's debts to the bank. She tried to have the guarantee reduced on the grounds that she had signed it at her husband's request, she had not read the document or had it explained to her and she had no formal education and was unfamiliar with commercial documents. The bank claimed that her error was unilateral and had not been induced by the bank. She claimed the guarantee was void as she had been in error about the nature of the document she was signing.

Court decision:

The contract was valid. The bank had not induced the error. Lord McCluskey said: "The law does not permit her to say that, because she did not take the trouble to read the document or ask for an explanation or to postpone signing it until she got one, she can now say that she thought the obligations she was undertaking were different from the ones which the document imposed upon her."

Exceptions include:

- ☐ **Gratuitous promises** – here the court may be willing to set these aside where the person who made the promise is in error.

- ☐ **Error of expression** – where parties have agreed terms, but the written document contains clerical errors. Court can now order rectification of documents under the Law Reform (Miscellaneous Provisions) (Scotland) Act 1985.

(iv) **Unilateral error induced by the other party** – where one party is in error about some essential of the contract and the error was brought about by something said or done by the other party. This is misrepresentation.

Exercise

Give examples of circumstances where contracts may be defined as void, voidable or unenforceable.

6

Misrepresentation

A contract may be set aside on the grounds of misrepresentation - provided certain conditions are fulfilled.

There must have been:

(i) A false statement of fact or fraudulent concealment of the true facts.

Statements of honestly held opinions or future intentions are not actionable as misrepresentations.

Flynn v Scott **1949 S.C. 442 (OH)**

Facts of the case:

Flynn bought a second-hand Bedford van from Scott, which Scott stated to be in good running order. The van broke down a week later and Flynn told Scott he was rejecting the van and repudiating the contract on the grounds that he had been induced to enter it because of Scott's misrepresentation.

Court decision:

Scott's statement was an expression of opinion and not a misrepresentation entitling Flynn to repudiate the contract.

Smith v Land and House Property Corporation **(1884) 28 Ch. D. 7**

Facts of the case:

Smith owned a hotel which he put up for sale, the particulars stating that the hotel was leased for the next 27 years to a Mr. Fleck, who was described as "a most desirable tenant." The corporation bought the hotel, but before completion Fleck became bankrupt and the corporation refused to complete the purchase. Smith sued for specific performance. It was shown that the tenant had not paid the most recent quarter's rent, and that the previous quarter's rent had only been paid after the landlord threatened proceedings against him. The corporation claimed that they only entered into the contract because of the statement that Fleck was a desirable tenant, and that Smith knew this to be untrue.

Court decision:

Specific performance would not be granted. The description of Fleck as a desirable tenant implied that Smith knew nothing to suggest that he was not. In fact Smith knew him as not a desirable tenant and this was a misrepresentation.

However concealing defects may be misrepresentation.

Gibson v National Cash Register Co Ltd **1925 S.C. 500**

Facts of the case:

Gibson brought an action against NCR on the ground that the company had sold him two cash registers and fraudulently concealed the fact that they were not new. Gibson was able to prove that he had wished to buy new machines and the company had held itself out as manufacturing and selling new machines. He also showed that the machines he was supplied with were secondhand but made to look like new by reconditioning.

Court decision:

Gibson had made out a *prima facie* case of fraudulent concealment.

Non-disclosure is not normally misrepresentation unless the contract is one of *uberrimae fidei* (of utmost good faith) such as an insurance contract:

The "Spathari" 1925 S.C. (HL) 6

Facts of the case:

Demetriades, a Greek shipbroker living in Glasgow, bought the SS Spathari with the intention of selling her to a Greek syndicate in Samos. Demetriades made arrangements with a Glasgow shipbroker called Borthwick that the ship should be transferred to Borthwick and registered and insured in his name, then sailed to Samos and there transferred to Demetriades. At the time Borthwick insured the ship, Greek ships were regarded as uninsurable, or only insurable for high premiums. Borthwick did not disclose to the insurance company Demetriades' interest in the ship. The ship sank off the coast of Portugal and the insurers refused to pay.

Court decision:

The insurance contract was void because of Borthwick's failure to disclose a material fact.

6

(ii) The false statement or concealment must be of a material nature i.e. it must go to the root of the contract. The contract will not be set aside if it relates to some trivial element of the contract.

(iii) The misrepresentation must have induced the other party to enter the contract. If it had no influence, the contract cannot be reduced.

Horsfall v Thomas (1862) 1 Hurl. & C. 90

Facts of the case:

The seller of a gun concealed the fact that it had a serious manufacturing defect by plugging the barrel. He failed to disclose this to the purchaser, who later tried to have the contract set aside on the basis of misrepresentation by fraudulent concealment.

Court decision:

The contract was valid. Although the actions of the seller amounted to fraudulent concealment, the buyer had not examined the gun before purchasing it, so the seller's misrepresentation had not induced the contract.

Exercise

What criteria must be fulfilled before an action can be successfully brought on the grounds that a contract was induced by misrepresentation?

Remedies

Remedies depend on the kind of misrepresentation:

(i) **Innocent**: where person makes an incorrect statement reasonably believing it to be true. The contract is void if misrepresentation resulted in fundamental error, otherwise it is voidable. Please note that the court will not set the contract aside unless parties can be restored to their original position (*restitutio in integrum*).

Boyd & Forrest v Glasgow and South Western Railway Co **1912 S.C. (HL) 93; 1915 S.C. (HL) 20**

Facts of the case:

The railway company invited tenders for construction of part of a railway line, and they showed to intending offerors a journal of bores supposedly taken along the proposed route. Boyd & Forrest won the tender, but when the work was in progress they discovered more rock and hard ground than had been indicated by the journal of bores. The data in the journal had been altered by one of the railway company's engineers, in the honest belief that some of the information supplied by the borers was incorrect. After completing the work, Boyd & Forrest sued the railway company for more than £100,000, the extra costs they had incurred on the contract, on the basis that they had been induced to enter the contract through the engineer's fraudulent misrepresentation.

Court decision:

There was no fraud. The engineer had only altered the information where he honestly believed it to be incorrect. The railway company then sued for the extra cost in damages, on the grounds that they had entered into the contract under essential error induced by innocent misrepresentation. There had been no misrepresentation. Further, if there was misrepresentation, Boyd & Forrest had failed to prove that it induced them to enter into the contract and, if it had, damages were not payable for innocent misrepresentation and the fact that *restitutio in integrum* was impossible excluded the remedy of reduction.

(ii) **Negligent**: where person does not intend to deceive but does not take proper care about the accuracy of the statement. The contract may again be void or voidable depending on whether the error is fundamental. Note that liability for negligent misrepresentation only arises where the party making the statement has a duty of care to make sure such statements are accurate. This duty comes under the law of delict and is discussed in Chapter 8.

Esso Petroleum v Mardon **[1976] Q.B. 801**

Facts of the case:

The parties were negotiating the lease of a petrol station. In the course of the negotiations, one of Esso's employees, with 40 years' experience of the trade, negligently misrepresented the likely sale of petrol from the station as 200,000 gallons per year. Mardon relied on this in entering the contract, which proved financially disastrous for him, with petrol sales reaching only 78,000 gallons in the first 15 months. Mardon claimed damages for negligent misrepresentation, while Esso argued that the statement had only been the expression of an opinion.

Court decision:

Esso had the necessary knowledge and skill to make such a statement, and had a duty of care to ensure the statement was reasonably correct. They were liable.

The Law Reform (Miscellaneous Provisions) (Scotland) Act 1985, s.10 clarified the position that damages for negligent misrepresentation could be claimed in Scotland.

(iii) **Fraudulent**: where person who made the misrepresentation did so with deliberate intent to deceive, or without any honest belief in the accuracy of the statement. Damages can always be claimed for fraudulent misrepresentation.

Morrisson v Robertson **1908 S.C. 332**

Facts of the case:

Morrisson had taken two cows to market for sale. He was approached by a man called Telford, who falsely claimed to be the son of Wilson, a farmer with whom Morrisson had had business dealings on a number of occasions. Telford claimed that he wished to buy the cows on behalf of his father and Morrisson let him take the cows on credit. Telford then sold the cows to Robertson, who bought them in good faith. Morrisson brought an action against Robertson in an attempt to recover the cows.

Court decision:

The contract between Morrisson and Telford was void owing to Morrisson's essential error as to the identity of the person with whom he was contracting. Telford could not therefore give title to the cows to Robertson, and Morrisson was entitled to reclaim them.

Macleod v Kerr **1965 S.C. 253**

Facts of the case:

Kerr advertised his Vauxhall car for sale. A man called Galloway answered the advertisement, giving his name as Craig, and he wrote a cheque in the name of Craig to pay for the car. The next day Kerr discovered that the cheque came from a stolen cheque book and he informed the police. In the meantime, Galloway, giving his name as Kerr, sold the car to Gibson, who owned a garage. The police took possession of the car from Gibson and Galloway was convicted of theft and fraud. The procurator fiscal brought an action of multiplepoinding (conflicting claims) to determine who was entitled to the car.

Court decision:

The contract between Kerr and Galloway was not void through essential error but was voidable. As it had not actually been avoided at the time of the sale to Gibson, Gibson got good title to the car.

Contract terms

■   General rules of interpretation

(a) Technical interpretation

Courts use certain rules to determine what words mean and what evidence is allowed. For example:

(i) Words and phrases are given ordinary everyday meaning unless an alternative meaning is clear.

(ii) Ambiguous words and phrases are interpreted to give effect to the agreement where possible.

(iii) Contracts which restrict freedom or exclude liability are interpreted strictly and *contra proferentem* (against the person putting it forward).

(iv) Where a contract has been reduced to writing, there is a presumption that the entire contract is contained in the written document.

At common law the extrinsic evidence rule was established via the following case.

Inglis v Buttery & Co **(1878) 5 R. (H.L.) 87**

Facts of the case:

Buttery & Co entered into a contract with Inglis under which Inglis was to carry out alterations and repairs to a steamship. The agreement was put into writing and signed by both parties. The written document stated that "The plating of the hull to be carefully overhauled and repaired, *but if any new plating is required, the same to be paid for extra.*"The words in italics were deleted by having a line drawn through them, though they could still be read. While carrying out the work, Inglis discovered that the hull plating was so badly worn that it had to be replaced. He claimed that Buttery & Co should have to pay extra for the new plating.

Court decision:

On an interpretation of the terms, Inglis had to supply the new plating under the contract price, and the court could not look at the deleted words or at any letters which had passed between the parties prior to execution of the written document in order to ascertain the intentions of the parties.

6

The statutory position was established via the Contract (Scotland) Act 1997 which allows extrinsic evidence to show the existence of terms outside the written document, unless the document itself states otherwise.

(b) Interpretation of the extent of the obligation

Where a contract is not reduced to writing, the court may have to decide whether a particular statement has become a term of the contract. The court will consider issues such as the importance placed on statement by person to whom it was made, the time between statement being made and formation of the final contract and the expertise of the person making the statement.

(c) Interpretation of the relative importance of terms

The terms in a contract may vary in their importance, i.e. important terms may be referred to as 'material' and less important ones as 'non-material terms '. Parties are free to stipulate that any term is to be regarded as material. If they do not, the courts decide by reference to the commercial importance of the clause and whether it goes to the fundamentals of the contract. Please note however that in some kinds of contract, certain terms are always regarded as being material. For example some material terms may be price, subject matter or quantity. As will be seen in Chapter 7, the remedies for material breach of contract differ from those for non-material breach.

> **Example**
>
> In most sales contracts where the value of the contract is high, the seller will generally make time of payment of the price an essential or material condition. Likewise time of delivery of goods or performance of a service may be specified in a contract as material.

■   Express, imported and implied terms

(a) Express terms

When we consider express terms we may think of them as terms stated and set out in the contract, i.e. this may be either in documents or in the oral statements of the parties.

(b) Imported terms

We can consider imported terms as another form of express term, which initially may not be set out in the contract itself, but may be incorporated by reference to another source. Note however in order to achieve the requirements of consensus parties must be aware of terms being imported or added to what they believe their obligations to be. A term is only regarded as imported if certain conditions are met:

(i) The term must be imported before or at the time the contract is made.

> *Olley v Marlborough Court Ltd* **[1949] 1 All E.R. 127**
>
> **Facts of the case:**
>
> A husband and wife arrived at a hotel as guests and paid for a room in advance. On one of the walls of their room was a notice: "The proprietors will not hold themselves responsible for articles lost or stolen unless handed to the manageress for safe custody." The wife closed the self-locking door of the bedroom and took the key down to the reception desk. Owing to inadequate supervision of the keyboard, a third party took the key and stole the wife's furs. When sued, the hotel tried to rely on the notice as a term of the contract.
>
> **Court decision:**
>
> The contract had been completed at the reception desk and no subsequent notices could import terms into it.

Thornton v Shoe Lane Parking **[1971] 2 Q.B. 163**

Facts of the case:

A notice outside a car park stated that cars were parked at owner's risk. Thornton, who had not parked at the car park before, took a ticket from the machine at the entrance and parked his car. The ticket, which Thornton did not read, stated in small print that it was issued subject to conditions. The conditions, displayed on a pillar opposite the ticket machine, exempted the company from liability for any injury to the customer. Thornton was injured when a concrete block fell on his car.

Court decision:

(a) The contract was concluded when the customer put his money in the machine, and the customer could not be bound by terms contained on the ticket, because the contract had already been concluded at that point. (b) Notice of the particular condition on which the defendants sought to rely had not been sufficiently brought to the attention of the customer, and therefore he was not bound by it.

But it will sometimes be regarded as having been imported through a course of dealing:

Spurling v Bradshaw **[1956] 2 All E.R. 121**

Facts of the case:

Spurling received goods he had ordered from Bradshaw, the goods being accompanied by a sales receipt which contained terms and conditions, one of which was an exemption of liability clause. The two parties had frequently dealt with each other in the past and Spurling had received many similar documents, but had never bothered to read them.

Court decision:

The terms and conditions on the receipt had been imported into the contract through a course of dealing between the parties. It made no difference if Spurling had actually read them.

(ii) The document containing terms to be imported must be regarded as a contractual document. The main factor is whether a reasonable person would assume the document to contain contractual terms.

Taylor v Glasgow Corporation **1952 S.C. 440**

Facts of the case:

Mrs. Taylor went to public baths in Glasgow. Having paid the price, she was given a ticket which she was required to hand over to the bath attendant. Printed on the front of the ticket were the words: "For conditions see other side" and on the back was printed: "The Corporation of Glasgow are not responsible for any loss injury or damage sustained by persons entering or using this establishment or its equipment." Mrs. Taylor knew there was printing on the ticket but did not read the condition. She fell and was badly injured, and brought an action for damages against the Corporation.

Court decision:

The ticket was merely a voucher which the pursuer would not have been expected to study for conditions; the conditions did not therefore form part of the contract.

(iii) The imported terms must have been brought to the notice of the other party.

Hood v The Anchor Line (Henderson Brothers) Ltd **1918 S.C. (HL) 143**

Facts of the case:

Hood was a passenger on 'The SS California', owned by the Anchor Line, on a voyage from New York to Glasgow. He was injured when being hoisted from a lifeboat after the ship ran aground off the Irish coast. The defenders claimed their liability was limited to £10 by a condition in the contract of carriage. The conditions were printed on part of the ticket retained by the passenger. Both the top and the foot of the document warned the passenger to read the terms and conditions, as did the envelope in which the ticket was given to the passenger. Mr. Hood had travelled with the Anchor Line on several occasions, but had never read the conditions, or noticed that conditions were attached.

Court decision:

The company had taken sufficient care to bring the conditions to the notice of the passenger. It did not matter that Hood had not actually read them, only that they had adequately been brought to his notice.

Williamson v North of Scotland and Orkney Steam Navigation Co **1916 S.C. 554**

Facts of the case:

Williams boarded the steamer at Scalloway and bought a return ticket to Aberdeen.

Court decision:

This was held not to be sufficient to bring the terms to the notice of a customer injured by negligence: "Nothing was done to direct attention to the condition printed on the face of the ticket in small type, which for any passenger must have been difficult to read, and for many passengers impossible to read without artificial assistance and very favourable surroundings."

The more unusual or onerous the term, the more effort must be made to bring them to the other party's attention:

Interfoto Picture Library Ltd v Stiletto Visual Programs **[1988] 1 All E.R. 348**

Facts of the case:

Stiletto required photographs from the 1950s for an advertising promotion and they requested Interfoto to supply these. Interfoto delivered 47 transparencies, together with a delivery note which stated the date by which the photos had to be returned. The note also contained a term which stated that a fee of £5 for each transparency would be payable for each day that they were retained after the return date. Stiletto forgot about the transparencies and did not return them until well after the deadline. Interfoto now claimed £3,783.50 under the clause in the conditions.

Court decision:

The clause was not imported into the contract because Interfoto had not done enough to bring it to the attention of Stiletto. Where a clause was very onerous, greater effort must be made to ensure it is brought to the notice of the other party. This decision was followed in the Scottish case of *Montgomery Litho Ltd v Maxwell* 2000 S.C. 56.

(c) Implied terms

Effectively we can say that implied terms are generally not agreed explicitly by the parties but are terms which the law will add to the contract. There are a variety of circumstances which will give rise to implied terms. For example:

(i) **Terms implied by trade custom**. These terms must be clear and well established via trade custom and are binding on the parties, even if they are not aware of them.

(ii) **Terms implied by certain relationships**. Even where not expressly agreed, standard terms will be assumed. For example it is implied that an employee is entitled to be paid.

(iii) **Terms implied to give business efficacy to a contract**. In certain circumstances the court may imply a term needed to make commercial sense of the contract.

The Moorcock **(1889) 14 P.D. 64**

Facts of the case:

A firm which owned a wharf charged a fee on cargo loaded onto or discharged from ships moored at their wharf on the Thames. Ships moored at the wharf had to lie on the river bed at low tide and the owners of the Moorcock were made aware of this when the contract between them and the wharf owners was made. While the Moorcock was discharging cargo at the jetty, the tide went out. The ship settled on a ridge of hard, uneven ground on the river bed and was badly damaged.

Court decision:

As the parties knew the ship would ground when the tide was low, and could be presumed to know that unless the ground was safe the ship would be in danger, there was an implied term that the owner of the wharf had a responsibility to ensure that the ground was safe.

(iv) **Terms implied by statute**. There is an increasing number of specific contracts which have terms implied into them by statutory provisions. The most common examples today are contracts which provide for the sale of goods (see for example section 2 of the Consumer Rights Act 2015) and employment contracts.

Terms implied at common law will be overridden by an express term which contradicts them. This is also true of some statutory implied terms, but some statutory implied terms cannot be excluded.

Unfair contract terms

Normally, it is up to the parties to a contract to strike a bargain, and the law does not interfere in the terms of that bargain. However, particularly where consumers contract with traders, the parties may be of different bargaining strengths. There are some provisions in the Consumer Rights Act 2015 which try to redress this. Under s.62, contract terms in consumer contracts must be fair, and unfair terms are not binding on the consumer. The statute provides a list of terms that will be automatically unfair in consumer contracts, and others that may be assessed for fairness. Under s.65, any clause in a consumer contract which purports to exclude liability for personal injury or death caused by negligence is void.

■ Rights under a contract

Privity of contract and its exceptions

Generally we can say that the rule is that no-one has rights under a contract unless he is a party to it. The next case is an example of the effects of privity of contract: the third party was the one that had suffered loss, and yet had no right to sue.

6

Blumer & Co v Scott & Sons **(1874) 1 R. 379**

Facts of the case:

The pursuers were shipbuilders who sold an unfinished ship to Ellis and Sons. The contract provided that delivery was not to be later than February 1872, "delays of engineers and every other unavoidable cause excepted." The pursuers then contracted with Scott and Sons, engineers, for the supply of engines for the ship; this contract provided that the engines were to be finished to the satisfaction of the pursuer's overseer. The engines were not delivered until October 1872. Both Blumer & Co and Ellis and Sons sued Scott for damages.

Court decision:

Blumer & Co were protected from liability to Ellis because of the exclusion clause in their contract. They were therefore not entitled to damages because they had suffered no loss. Ellis and Sons, on the other hand, had no claim against Scott because they were not a party to the contract for supplying the engines and the terms of that contract were not such as to confer a *jus quaesitum tertio* (third party right) on them (see next section).

Exceptions:

(a) Third party right *(jus quaesitum tertio).*

However there are some circumstances in which a third party is entitled to enforce a contract when it specifically confers on him a **third party right** or *jus quaesitum tertio*. His rights are in addition to those of the existing parties. For this right to arise, the following requirements must be met:

- ☐ There must be an **express intention to benefit** the third party;
- ☐ This must be **irrevocable**;
- ☐ The **third party must be identified** in the contract;
- ☐ A *jus quaesitum tertio* **must be created by contract** and not by a unilateral promise.

A leading case is *Carmichael v Carmichael's Executrix.*

Carmichael v Carmichael's Executrix **1920 S.C. (HL) 195.**

Facts of the case:

A life insurance policy was taken out by Carmichael on the life of his son. The terms provided that if the son died after the age of 21, from which age he would pay the premiums, the insurance company would pay out. The son died at the age of 21, but before he paid any premiums. The father had paid the premiums from when the son was aged 8 to the time of his death. A dispute ensured between the father, who considered himself entitled to the benefit of the policy, and the son's heir.

Court decision:

The court recognised a *jus quaesitum tertio* in this case and awarded the money to the heir rather than the father.

It should be noted that a similar (though not identical) right has been introduced in England by statute recently. Also, the Scottish Law Commission has proposed that this area of law should be reformed.

It should be noted that a similar (though not identical) right has been introduced in England by statute recently. Also, the Scottish Law Commission has proposed that this area of law should be reformed.

(b) Agency

Where contract is made by an agent acting for a principal, the principal acquires the rights and obligations under the contract.

(c) Assignation

A third party may be able to obtain rights under a contract by having it assigned to him. Effectively we can say that this makes him a party to the contract in place of the original party. Please note however that the assignee has no better rights than the person who assigned the contract to him. Further, an assignation has no effect until the other party to the contract has been informed. Contracts with an element of *delectus personae* (choice of the person) cannot be assigned.

Scottish Widows Fund v Buist **(1876) 3 R. 1078**

Facts of the case:

In 1871 a life policy was taken out for £1000, the policy containing the usual stipulations that it would be void if any untrue statements had been made concerning the assured's state of health or age. In 1872 the policy was assigned to Buist and others, and the assignation was intimated to the insurance company. In 1875 the assured died and the assignees of the policy claimed for payment of the £1000. The insurance company raised an action of reduction on the grounds that the assured had knowingly misrepresented his state of health.

Court decision:

The assignees were subject to any exceptions and defences which could have been pleaded against the assured. The false statements were a relevant ground of reduction against the assignees of the policy.

6

(d) Transmission

When a person dies or becomes bankrupt, his contractual rights and obligations pass to his executor (on death) or trustee (on bankruptcy). Note however that contracts involving *delectus personae* do not transmit.

Contracts concluded electronically

■ Background

People might believe that it is a legal requirement that all contracts must be written and witnessed to provide validity. However, as seen in Chapter 5, under Scots law most contracts do not in fact require such formalities. Contracts may be verbal or can be established by looking at the parties' behaviour or by implication (see for example *Carlill v Carbolic Smokeball*

Company, 1893 or *Thornton v Shoe Lane Parking,* 1971). These contracts will generally be evidenced via statements or testimony from the parties involved and their witnesses.

■   Why regulate e-commerce?

Electronic commerce or e-commerce is generally the term applied to commercial transactions concluded on-line or via email. In the UK, electronic commerce is regulated by the Electronic Commerce (EC Directive Regulations 2002/ SI 2013, which enacts the Electronic Commerce Directive (2000/31/EC) into UK law. The regulations apply where the goods or services are provided online, for example software or music downloads and also where they are ordered on-line but provided by the physical delivery of the goods, DVDs, books etc.

It is generally accepted that the main advantages of trading on-line for businesses are that it provides access to a wider customer base, provides the opportunity to offer more specialised or tailored goods or services, and has lower start-up costs. Having similar rules across the 28 member states of the European Union allows both traders and consumers to be more confident about making cross-border contracts.

E-commerce regulations aim to regulate providers of 'information society services'. This term covers: *"any service normally provided for remuneration, at a distance, by means of electronic equipment for the processing (including digital compression) and storage of data, and at the individual request of a recipient of the service"* *(Reg 2* with reference to recital *17 of* the Electronic Commerce Directive *2000).*

This broad concept covers most on-line commercial activities including:

1   The on-line sale of goods and services.

2   The activities of Internet Service Providers (ISPs) and email providers who enable access to the internet and email.

3   On-line or email advertising.

Please note that for the E-Commerce Regulations to apply, all elements of this definition must be fulfilled, therefore face to face transactions will be excluded on the basis and need for the 'distance' service provision. Services which are not provided at the individual request of the recipient will also be excluded (note the *consensus in idem* requirement here).

The Electronic Contracts (EC Directive) Regulations 2002 set out rules which traders must follow when transacting, to make sure that the basic information is provided to the other contracting party including who the service provider is, the address, the email address, any trade body the service provider is a member of, any relevant codes of practice that the trader is covered by, the VAT number if registered, and a clear indication of the price. Information about the technical steps to be taken to make a contract online should be provided, including a means for correcting input errors. Commercial communications must be clearly marked as such.

Electronic contracts

At the outset we need to understand the importance of establishing who the offeror is and who the offeree is. Further, when trading electronically we need to determine at what point the contract is concluded. This point is especially important when trading cross-border, as we need to understand not only the point at which the contract is made but also which of the countries' courts may have jurisdiction and which laws are applicable. The Electronic Commerce Directive does not clarify the issue.

Please note it is not clear whether or not the 'postal rule' discussed in Chapter 5 applies in electronic commerce. However there are a few cases involving telexes that establish that an acceptance is binding only when it is received: (see for example *Entores v Miles Far East Corp* [1955] 2 Q.B. 327 and *Brinkibon v Stahag Stahl und Stahlwarenhandelsgesellschaft mbH* [1983] 2 A.C. 34).

Telex technology is not the same as digital communication, and it is possible to argue that the postal rule applies to digital communication. This point would need to be clarified by the trader prior to contracts being made. This may be part of the initial negotiations.

One further issue not clarified by the Directive is whether goods shown on a web-site are 'an invitation to treat' or an 'offer for sale'. This should be clarified on the web-site. If it is not done, then potentially if the wrong price is displayed, the seller lays itself open to purchasers insisting that they have accepted an offer at that price. Good practice should prompt the seller to clarify this in his terms and conditions and should make the purchaser click to indicate they have read and accepted them, and only then should they be able to progress to make an offer.

6

■   ## Electronic signatures

Section 7 of the Electronic Communications Act 2000 provides that electronic signatures may now be incorporated into electronic documents and are now admissible as evidence in court. The Requirements of Writing (Scotland) Act 1995 has now been amended to provide that contracts which require formal validity may now be concluded electronically, where the granter has authenticated the electronic document by adding his digital signature and this signature is certified in accordance with the act. See ss.1(2A), 2A and 3A of the Requirements of Writing (Scotland) Act 1995 as amended by the Automated Registration of Title to Land (Electronic Communication) (Scotland)Order 2006 SS1 2006/491, made under section 8 of the Electronic Communications Act 2000.

This effectively means that all contracts under Scots law can be entered into electronically where there has been compliance with the provisions of the Requirements of Writing (Scotland) Act 1995.

Further reading

Black, G., (2015) *Business Law in Scotland* Edinburgh: W. Green 3rd Edition Chapter 4.

Black, G., (2014) *Woolman on Contract* 5th Edition Edinburgh: W. Green, Chapters 6-9.

MacQueen, H, and Garland, C., (2015) Signatures in Scots Law: Form, Effect and Burden of Proof. *Juridical Review,* **2**, 107-134.

MacQueen, H., and Thomson, J., (2012) *Contract Law in Scotland* 3rd Edition Haywards Heath: Bloomsbury Professional, Chapter 3.

7 Extinction of Contractual Obligations and Breach of Contract

Yvonne McLaren

Over the previous chapters we have seen that by engaging within a voluntary agreement or contract we may incur a variety of rights and obligations. Generally we may view rights as protective in that they may afford us certain legal protections, i.e. we can see for example that unfair contract terms may enable the party to withdraw from the obligations which the contract confers. It is important to note that such terms are generally considered on a case-by-case basis, although we do have statutory protections, most notably via the Consumer Rights Act 2015 in relation to unfair terms, under which certain terms are automatically unfair and void in consumer contracts, other terms are on the list of unfair terms, and yet others may be examined to see if they are unfair.

In the absence of any concerns or issues associated with the formation of the contract or its contents, most contracts will likely be performed without issue and the relationship between the parties will continue as before. Below is a discussion of the various ways in which obligations may be generally concluded. The chapter ends with a discussion of the remedies for breach of contract.

Extinction of contractual obligations

■ Performance or agreement

Fundamental to our understanding of contract law is the requirement that any contract will have at least two parties. These parties will have corresponding rights and obligations to one another, i.e. they may be seen as both creditor and debtor to one another, where a debt may not necessarily be an obligation to pay money: it can equally be a duty to perform. An example of this may be seen within a general contract of employment. Here the employer will have a duty to pay his employee for performance of contractual obligations, while the employee will have a corresponding right to that payment for the duties he has performed.

When these reciprocal arrangements are fulfilled, the contract is terminated because the obligations have been carried out, i.e. performance is complete. Generally we can say that the vast majority of contracts which take place on a day to day basis are terminated, without dramatic occurrence, by performance.

However, there are other ways by which a contract may come to an end: as discussed in Chapter 6, a void contract cannot be ended because technically it never existed. Nevertheless a court may have to declare that the contract is void and make judgement regarding the respective rights of the parties.

A voidable contract continues to exist unless or until it is set aside. Please note that it is the court that sets the contract aside and not the parties themselves. If third parties acquire rights under a voidable contract in good faith and for value, then that contract cannot be set aside.

In the interests of consumer protection, there are circumstances in which the law allows for the party with the obligation to be released from that obligation. See for example The Consumer Contracts (Information Cancellation and Additional Charges) Regulations 2013. These regulations allow consumers to cancel contracts which have been made during a visit by a trader to a consumer's home or place of work. The trader cannot enforce the contract unless the consumer was given written notice of the right to cancel within fourteen days and a statutory cancellation form. The consumer is free to cancel the contract within the time limit.

Tip

The general rule in bilateral contracts is that if one party completely fails to perform the obligations contained within the contract then the other party need not perform at all. We can define this in terms of the 'mutuality principle' under which the obligations of the parties to a contract are generally regarded as reciprocal.

This point is best illustrated by the case of:

Graham v United Turkey Red Co. Ltd **1922 S.C. 533**

Facts of the case

Graham had a contract of agency with United under which he was required to sell goods for United. Contained within the contract was a restrictive covenant, which prevented Graham from selling the goods from other manufacturers. Graham started to sell the goods of rivals. His contract was terminated and he sued Turkey for commission he believed he was owed.

Court decision

The court held that if a party to a contract ceases to perform the contract according to its terms, he is entitled to commission up to the point when the breach occurred but under the mutuality principle, not in respect of work done after the breach.

7

It is important to note that the general rule is however subject to the following exceptions:

☐ A *severable contract* may consist of several independent obligations. It is therefore possible that a party who performs only some of these obligations may claim in respect of those performed, but will remain liable in damages for the obligations not performed. Please note that whether or not a contract is severable may depend on the intentions of the parties.

☐ Any party who had completed a large proportion of the contractual obligations may be said to have made *substantial performance*. Please note this will be decided on a case by case basis and the other party can insist that the party performs the contract. By failing to do so the party will remain liable in damages.

☐ *Voluntary acceptance* of partial performance may allow for a claim based on unjustified enrichment: i.e. the value or benefit received by a person at the expense of another who suffered the loss of the benefit.

☐ *Prevention of performance* by one of the contract parties may allow the party who was prevented from performing their obligations to make a claim based on unjustified enrichment.

■ Novation

We can define this as the *substitution of a new agreement for an existing one*, or the substitution of a new debtor or creditor for an existing one, with the agreement of both parties, in such a way as to make clear that the original agreement is terminated. An example of this might be a fruit seller who now supplies pears instead of apples to the other party. It is important that the original obligation is expressly discharged, as there is a general presumption in law against novation since there is a danger that one of the parties may find himself with two obligations to perform.

■ Delegation

Effectively we can say that delegation is really a form of novation. It involves the substitution of a new debtor, as distinct from an entirely new obligation, in place of the original. It requires the express consent of the creditor. Please note that it would be inappropriate in a contract which has an element of *delectus personae* or choice of person. An example of this might be an agent, where because his appointment is a matter of personal confidence, has no implied authority to delegate the performance of his duties. Traditionally in law we might use the legal maxim which states "*delegatus non potest delegare*" in other words the one to whom delegation has been made cannot delegate. There may however be exceptions to the general rule where for example it is well recognised that a solicitor in Scots law may delegate the searching of public registers to a professional searcher or an architect may delegate measurement of final plans to a surveyor.

■ Frustration

Frustration, from the Latin *'frustra'* or in vain can terminate a contract which is valid and at least in theory can be performed, but subsequent events (usually outwith the control of either party), have made the end result of performance significantly different from the original intention of the parties to the contract.

Generally the concept of frustration may be illustrated by two cases which are commonly referred to as the 'coronation cases' due to sickness and the subsequent difficulties which arose from the postponement of the coronation of Edward VII.

Krell v Henry [1903] 2K.B. 740 (CA)

Facts of the case:

A contract was formed for the two-day hire of rooms in Pall Mall for £75 to overlook the coronation procession. The king became ill and the coronation had to be postponed.

Court decision

In theory it would have been possible for the contract to be performed, i.e. the hiring of the room, but the outcome of looking at the London traffic rather than the procession would have been so radically different from what the parties originally intended as to frustrate the contract.

Contrast this with the case of Herne Bay, again resulting from the postponement of the coronation of King Edward VII, although it is worth noting that both cases may be considered when deciding if frustration is applicable.

7

Herne Bay Steamboat Co. v Hutton [1903] 2 K.B. 683(CA)

Facts of the case:

There was a contract for the hire of a pleasure boat to watch the review of the fleet off Spithead by the king. Although the king was unable to attend and the review was cancelled, the fleet was still there and it was possible to enjoy the special outing.

Court decision

The contract was held not to have been frustrated because the foundation of the contract i.e. the hiring of the boat had not become radically different.

When might we consider that a contract is not frustrated?

☐ **Difficulty in performance**. A contract will not become frustrated merely because it becomes more difficult to perform. For example if a contract determines that goods must be carried on a particular ship and that ship sinks then we may conclude it has become frustrated because the ship has sunk. However if the parties merely wish that the goods be carried by a particular route it will not be frustrated if this becomes impossible, as long as the goods can be carried by a different route.

□ **A** *force majeure* **clause** in a contract sets out what should happen if unexpected difficulties should arise. Such clauses are given legal effect and provide for the situation where both parties may escape liability or obligation when an extraordinary event or circumstance beyond the control of the parties takes place. Examples may include war, strikes, riot, crime or an event described by legal terms as an '*act of God* 'such as a hurricane, flooding, earthquake, volcanic eruption etc.

□ **The 'frustrating' event was foreseeable**, i.e. a party who foresees, or should have foreseen, a particular event cannot claim that this event frustrates the contract.

□ **The 'frustrating' event was self-induced**, i.e. a party who brought about an event that would ordinarily frustrate the contract, cannot claim that the event has frustrated the contract.

■ The legal effects of frustration

The legal effect of frustration is to relieve both parties of liability for further performance or the contract. In the case of frustration, impossibility or illegality, it is possible that money may have been paid in advance.

Cantiere San Rocco SA v Clyde Shipbuilding & Engineering Co. **1923 S.C. (HL) 105**

Facts of the case:

A Scottish company had agreed to supply engines to an Austrian company, payment to be by instalments. The first instalment was paid just prior to the outbreak of the First World War. No engines were supplied as the outbreak of war made performance of the contract illegal. After the war ended the Austrian company raised an action for recovery of the first instalment.

Court decision:

The House of Lords allowed recovery on appeal. The rule of restitution would only apply (note this was part of unjustified enrichment) to the effect that where a payment had been made under a valid contract which became frustrated by supervening illegality, the payment would be recoverable on the ground that the reason for making the payment had failed.

Breach of contract

As previously stated the majority of contracts are performed without any problematic events but realistically there will always be occasions where we will have defaulters i.e. those unwilling to perform their obligations. Effectively we can say that when one of the parties to a contract fails to carry out his side of the obligation, he will be considered in breach of contract, unless the reasons for his non-performance are recognised as valid in law. An example of this may be supervening impossibility.

Breach can arise, effectively in three different ways:

1 total non-performance,

2 partial performance, or

3 defective performance.

This infers a situation where 'the innocent party' may be caught unaware of any problems with performance. However there is another form of breach where there may be circumstances in which one of the parties could indicate in advance of performance, by his words or actions that he does not intend to fulfil his obligations. This is known as **anticipatory breach**.

7

Example of anticipatory breach:

A famous singer has been booked to perform on the 31st December at the Edinburgh New Year or 'Hogmanay' celebrations. On the 1st of December she states that she will not be coming. She is saying, in effect that on the 31st December she will be in breach of contract. The question then becomes, what remedies would be open to the promoter?

The promoter will have two choices: (1) He could treat this as a repudiation of the contract by the singer and could thus rescind, on the grounds of material breach, and claim damages; (2) He could wait until the time of performance and see what happens. In this option of course there is no rescission and the contract is effectively kept 'alive'. If the singer changes her mind and turns up to perform on the 31st December, it goes without saying that there is no breach of contract.

Please note for an anticipatory breach to take place, the refusal to fulfil the obligation must be definite by the party. If one party merely expresses doubts about his ability to perform, that is not anticipatory breach. If in such circumstances, the other party then attempts to rescind, that party could be liable for damages.

White & Carter (Councils) Ltd. v McGregor **[1962] AC 413; 1962 S.C. (HL) 1**

Facts of the case:

White supplied street litter bins to local authorities on the condition that White could sell advertising space on the bins. One of White's representatives called at McGregor's garage to arrange a new advertising contract which was to last for three years. Terms were agreed with the garage manager and the contract was established. Later that day, McGregor telephoned White to cancel the contract. White chose to ignore this purported cancellation. They prepared the advertisements and displayed them for the three year period.

Court decision:

White & Carter were held to have been entitled to proceed with the contract and to sue for the contract price, even though McGregor had already intimated that he would not perform his side of the obligation.

Please note that this case has not been without its critics, with the English courts showing a reluctance to follow this decision. The main criticism has been that the decision appears to ignore the principle of mitigation, discussed later in this chapter. See for example *Clea Shipping Co. v Bulk Oil International (The Alaskan Trader)* [1984] 1 All E.R. 129, where it was held that the innocent party's keeping a ship at anchor off Piraeus for seven months after an anticipatory breach, was wholly unreasonable.

However the court decision in White & Carter was followed in this case.

Salaried Staff London Loan Co. Ltd v Swears & Wells **1985 S.C. 189**

Facts of the case:

Tenants had taken a 34-year lease of premises on an industrial estate but after the lease had run for only five years, the tenants gave notice that they wished to renounce it.

Court decision:

The court held that only in exceptional circumstances would the court decline to enforce the legal rights of the innocent party. Please note that the court also indicated that what is meant by 'exceptional' would be for the courts themselves to decide on a case by case basis.

■   Material and non-material breaches

Some breaches of contract are more serious than others. If there is no performance at all, or the performance differs markedly from that contracted for, that would be material breach. As shown in Chapter 6, sometimes people expressly state in the contract which provisions will be regarded as material. More trivial breaches of contract are non-material. Where there has been material breach, the party in breach is said to have *repudiated* the contract.

If a court considers there has been material breach of contract, more remedies are available than for non-material breach. If a contract has been repudiated by the material breach of one of the parties, the other party can rescind the contract. This results in freeing the party who rescinds the contract from further obligations under the contract. However, the decision in *Wade v Waldon* 1909 S.C. 571 points to the what happens if the 'innocent party' wrongly second-guesses what a court might do and rescinds a contract in which the court later determines that the breach was non-material.

Wade v Waldon **1909 S.C. 571**

Facts of the case:

A comedian contracted to appear in two Glasgow theatres for a week. His contract obliged him to supply advance publicity material. When he failed to do that, the management of the theatres cancelled his show, on the grounds of the comedian's material breach of contract. He then offered to do the show, but this was not accepted by the theatre management. Consequently, the comedian sued the theatre company for damages for its breach of contract.

Court decision:

The failure to deliver the publicity material was held *not* to be material breach, and therefore rescission of the contract was not justified. Consequently, the failure to allow the comedian to perform was itself repudiation, justifying a claim of damages by the comedian.

7

■   Other remedies for breach of contract

Here the innocent party may consider what he feels best for his particular circumstance and how he wishes to proceed. The main remedies and defensive measures are specific implement and interdict, rescission, retention, lien or action for payment, and damages. These will now be examined below.

Specific implement

This is a remedy which requires that a person performs his obligations. The innocent party will ask the court for a decree to make the party in breach fulfil the terms of his obligation under the contract, i.e. the court will be asked to award a decree *ad factum praestandum* which means "for the performance of an act". This award asks that the party specifically implements his contractual obligations.

Specific implement is, in theory, the primary remedy to which an innocent party is entitled in the case of breach of contract. However, it is not a particularly common remedy and it is important to consider that there are a number of situations where the courts do not consider specific implement an equitable or suitable remedy and will not grant a decree as a matter of course. Generally this type of award is used to enforce obligations against the seller of heritable property (land and/or buildings).

The following are the main areas where a court will not grant a decree of specific implement:

☐ Where the obligation is to pay a sum of money. Generally as a matter of public policy a creditor can enforce payment by simpler processes, such as an action for payment or diligence (process of enforcement of obligations).

☐ Where a contract involves personal relationships.

☐ Where the subject matter of the contract has no special significance in itself. An action of specific implement could be appropriate if the contract itself concerned a specific item such as a unique painting which might be said to have a *pretium affectionis* or price of affection.

☐ Where the contract is illegal or impossible to perform or where the court could not enforce the decree.

☐ Where in the opinion of the court, it would be unjust to grant such a remedy.

Note that in England the equivalent remedy is specific performance.

Interdict

Effectively, an interdict is asking the court to prevent someone doing something: if an action is negative then the court will award decree to stop the party in breach from doing something he agreed not to do.

> **Example**
>
> Ann worked for Bill under a contract containing a restrictive covenant which prohibited her using Bill's customer and price lists to seek customers for any other business after leaving her job. Ann left her job and immediately set up a rival business, making use of Bill's list of customers to offer them similar goods at lower prices.
>
> In this example, interdict would be a suitable remedy. Damages might also be appropriate.

Please note that interdict can never be used to enforce a positive obligation.

Retention and lien

The right of retention, or lien as it is known in English law, is the withholding of payment of a money debt until the other party performs his obligations in full. For example a tenant may withhold his payment of rent until the landlord carries out his legal duty to put the house or apartment into habitable condition.

There are restrictions as to when this measure can be used since as a general rule of law a debtor cannot refuse to pay a debt simply because he has another claim again the creditor. Please note that retention may be viewed as more a defensive measure rather than a remedy, in that it suspends performance.

Lien is the withholding of property which would normally be delivered to the other party. Effectively we have two kinds of lien, general and special. The special lien is generally the more common of the two and allows a person who has done work on the moveable property of another, or who has not been paid for the work to retain possession of that property until he has received the payment which is due. The most common example often given is that of the car mechanic who repairs another party's car and has the right to payment. If this is not given then it may be appropriate that the garage retain the car until payment is made. A general lien may be described as the right to withhold or detain the property of another, in respect of any debt which happens to be due by the proprietor, or for a general balance of accounts arising on a particular train of employment. Effectively we can see examples of this mostly within the banking and legal sectors, where the work completed on behalf of a client may give rise to the banker or lawyer using a general lien in order to obtain payment for multiple obligations.

7

For example, a solicitor may choose to retain the title deeds to heritable property (land or buildings), for example, until payment for his services are forthcoming.

Two issues must be noted:

1 Lien is a possessory right so that in the example above the car does not become the property of the garage, it is merely in the garage's possession.

2 A special lien can only be exercised against the goods in which are specific or special to the contract.

Damages

In considering the notion of damages, it is often the words of Lord President Inglis, in the case of *Webster & Co. v Cramond Iron Co.* (1875) 2 R. 752, which are quoted i.e. *"it is impossible to say that a contract can be broken, even in respect of time, without the party being entitled to claim damages - at the lowest, nominal damages."*

Scots law provides that wherever there is an established breach of contract, however small and no matter what other remedies or measures have been used by the pursuer, a claim for damages is always possible. The purpose of damages is to compensate the innocent party for his loss and to effectively put him back into the position he would have been in, had the contract been fully performed, in so far as money alone is capable of doing.

Please note that the actual breach of contract must have caused the pursuer some loss. Even if no actual loss has been sustained the court may award nominal damages to compensate for the trouble and inconvenience endured.

Points relevant to damages include:

☐ **Damages are never to be considered as a penalty** or civil punishment of the party in breach. In other words Scots law does not encourage 'punitive' damages as the fundamental purpose of the damages is to compensate the innocent party for any losses incurred.

☐ **The innocent party is expected to take 'reasonable steps' to minimise his loss**, i.e. damages will not be claimable in respect of losses that could have been mitigated, as can be seen in the following case.

Gunter & Co v Lauritzen **(1894) 1 S.L.T. 435**

Facts of the case:

Lauritzen had agreed to sell a cargo of Dutch hay to Gunter who intended to resell the hay in consignments to his customers. Lauritzen failed to supply goods of the required quality but when he was sued for damages he claimed that Gunter could have obtained the goods elsewhere and that it had not minimised its loss.

Court decision:

The court held the even though the commodity was in scare supply and could only be bought in small amounts the minimisation of loss did not require such an onerous demand. In other words the innocent party was only required to take reasonable steps.

☐ **Remoteness**: The courts will only allow loss which is a direct and foreseeable result of the breach of contract to be claimed. Damages in that case may be referred to as 'general' or 'ordinary' damages. However if there are 'knock-on' circumstances which lead to an unusual or special loss, the party in breach is not held liable but please note that if the defender has been made aware of those circumstances this may lead to liability. See for example the next case.

Hadley v Baxendale **(1854) 9 Ex. 341**

Facts of the case:

Hadley's flour mill was at a standstill because the cast-iron crankshaft from a steam engine had fractured. Hadley hired the carriers Baxendale to transport it to a foundry for repair. Hadley told Baxendale that the shaft must be sent immediately and Baxendale promised to deliver it the next day. Baxendale did not know that the mill would be inoperable until the new shaft arrived.

Court decision:

It was held that Baxendale was negligent and caused a delay in delivering the new crankshaft. The company was in breach of contract, since it had undertaken to complete the work in two days. However Hadley was not entitled to claim special damages for the loss of profits when the mill was at a standstill because these special circumstances had not been properly explained to Baxendale, i.e. the losses were not foreseeable.

Balfour Beatty Construction (Scotland) Ltd v Scottish Power plc **1994 S.C. (HL) 20**

Please note this case involves the application of the rules in *Hadley v Baxendale* as previously discussed.

Facts of the case:

Balfour had contracted with Scottish Power for a temporary supply of electricity to make concrete for the construction of an aqueduct for the Union Canal in Edinburgh. A disruption in supply led to the construction being demolished and rebuilt at loss to Balfour. Balfour then sued Scottish Power. The issue was whether Scottish Power could be held to have foreseen the potential consequences of a loss of power.

Court decision:

The Outer House of the Court of Session held that Scottish Power could not be imputed to have this knowledge. This was reversed by the Inner House on appeal.

The House of Lords held that technical knowledge could not be imputed to Scottish Power which had not been expressly given it by Balfour, and therefore the damages claim failed.

Amount of damages awarded

When we think of damages it is better to think of them as attempting to put an individual into the position they would have been in, had the contract been fulfilled. We therefore generally talk of damages as reparation rather than compensation. Subject to the rules of causation and remoteness, damages may be claimed for matters such as loss of profit, damages that become payable to a third party, and the cost of putting right defects caused by the breach of contract.

Solatium

In Scots law, damages are generally not recoverable for injured feelings or distress but if the whole purpose of the contract was to provide enjoyment and relaxation then it may be possible for damages that are claimed for disappointment and distress which are a direct result of breach of contract. Effectively we can discuss this as a payment or other recompense for mental suffering or financial or other loss.

Example

Andy and Jane went on a package holiday to Greece. The brochure stated that the hotel had a pool, that there were free excursions daily, and a full entertainment pro-gramme in the evenings. In reality the pool had not yet been built, the excursions were in fact very expensive, and there was entertainment only on the final evening. The resort was extremely noisy and Andy and Jane got very little sleep. They consider they had had the 'holiday from hell' and felt very angry and upset by the experience.

These are the kinds of circumstances where solatium might be appropriate. Similar problems arose in *Jarvis v Swans Tours Ltd* [1973] Q.B. 233 and the court recognised it was appropriate to award damages for the lost enjoyment of the holiday.

Agreed damages (liquidated damages)

It is not uncommon in today's commercial environment that the contract itself may in fact state what damages should be sought in the event of breach of that contract. In other words, as part of the negotiation, it may be the case that both parties have decided on a fiscal amount. Whether this agreement is given effect will depend upon whether the amount agreed may be defined as liquidated damages or a penalty.

Liquidated damages are effectively a genuine 'pre-estimate' of the loss which the parties believe any breach will incur. Effectively these liquidated damages are applied even if the loss was not the amount spelt out in the liquidated damages clause. Excessive sums which suggest penalty or a dis-proportionate response from the other party may not represent a genuine pre-estimate of the loss. These may be known as penalties and in the pursuit of good faith may be set aside by the courts in the appropriate circumstances. When deciding if a penalty exists the court may pay regard to the principles set out, as per Lord Dunedin in the following case:

Dunlop Pneumatic Tyre Co. v New Garage and Motor Co. [1915] **A.C. 79**

■ The uses of the words 'penalty' or 'liquidate damages' is not conclusive in itself

■ A penalty punishes; liquidate damages are a genuine pre-estimate of loss

■ Whether a sum is a penalty or liquidate damages is a question judged at the formation of the contract, not at the time of the alleged breach

■ If a sum is clearly extravagant, it will be counted as penal and thus unenforceable

■ If the same single lump sum is payable on the occurrence of several different situations, it will be presumed to be penal.

This issue has recently been ruled upon in the Supreme Court in the case of *Makdessi v Cavendish Square Holdings BV.*

Makdessi v Cavendish Square Holdings BV **[2015] U.K.S.C. 67.**

Facts of the case:

The case concerned a contract to sell a stake in a holding company in which Makdessi had considerable goodwill. The contract therefore included time-limited restrictive covenants, imposing very expensive consequences for breach. There was also a provision that in the event of a breach of the restrictive covenants, the buyer would acquire an option to purchase the remaining shares at a price that excluded goodwill. Makdessi then breached the restrictive covenants, and contended that the clauses were penalty clauses and unenforceable. The Court of Appeal had agreed, but the Supreme Court took a different view.

Court decision:

The Supreme Court held that rather than just focus on whether the clause was a genuine pre-estimate of loss, as in the previous case law, such as *Dunlop* above, the obligations should be broken down into primary obligations, (to tender some kind of performance) which would not be reviewable, and secondary obligations (to pay a particular sum in damages) which could be reviewed. They reviewed these clauses, which had been drafted by experienced commercial lawyers, and declared that the test in these cases where the liquidate damages are extreme, is whether the secondary obligation imposes a detriment out of all proportion to any legitimate interest the innocent party might have in enforcement of the primary obligation, given that damages are not meant to be a punishment.

The Supreme Court considered that the test of genuine pre-estimate of loss (as in *Dunlop*) still applied to simple liquidate damages cases, but not where the penalties were unconscionable. Where parties were of equal bargaining strength, the presumption was that they were the best judges of what terms should be included in their contract. In this case, however, the Supreme Court held that these restrictive covenants and the price formula for the sale of the shares, were not penalties and were therefore valid, in the circumstances of the case.

Note, restrictive covenants were discussed in Chapter 5.

Time limits on remedies

The Prescription and Limitation (Scotland) Act 1973 provides that in most cases remedies for breach of contract must be used within five years of the right to sue arising. The making of a claim or acknowledgment that a claim exists will naturally interrupt the prescriptive period.

Exercise

Ann contracted with Fred for him to landscape her garden. Fred claimed to have a certificate in horticulture and extensive experience in garden design. The work was done very slowly and it became apparent as the work progressed that Fred had never done this work before. The garden is now a sea of mud, and empty of all plants. Fred has presented his invoice for the work.

In relation to the law on breach of contract, advise Ann as to which remedies might be appropriate here.

Unjustified enrichment

In some cases when a contract has been terminated, but there are outstanding issues relating to that contract, unjustified enrichment may be used in order to seek a remedy if there is no remedy in the law of contract. An example of this may be seen in frustration or if one of the parties prevented further performance of the contract or where one party voluntarily accepted partial performance of the contract or where the contract did not provide how much should be paid.

7

Dollar Land (Cumbernauld) Ltd. v CIN Properties Ltd. **1998 S.C. (HL) 90**

Facts of the case:

Dollar were developers of a shopping centre and claimed unjustified enrichment in relation to the irritation of leases by their landlords, as a result of which Dollar had suffered loss of a portion of rent that they had been allowed to retain from rent paid by their subtenants.

Court decision:

The court held that unjustified enrichment could be claimed where (1) the defenders had been unjustifiably enriched at the pursuer's expense, (2) there is no legal justification for the enrichment and (3) it would be equitable to address the enrichment. Note however that in this case even though there was enrichment, in this case there was justification in that there was express provision contained within the terms of the lease. The provision could therefore not be said to be unjust.

Conclusion

On a day-to-day basis contracts will be established and will conclude with both parties being completely satisfied with the interaction. We have seen above that there may be times when we need to rely more on legal measures to support the parties in coming to a positive conclusion.

Further reading

Black, G., (ed) (2015) *Business Law in Scotland* 3rd edition, Edinburgh: W. Green 3rd Edition. Chapter 4.

Black, G., (2014) *Woolman on Contract* 5th edition Edinburgh: W. Green. Chapters 10 and 13.

MacNeil, I (2014) *Scots Commercial Law*. Edinburgh; Avizandum Publishing Ltd. MacQueen, H., and Thomson, J., (2012) *Contract Law in Scotland* 3rd edition Hayward's Heath: Bloomsbury Professional. Chapters 4, 5 and 6.

Richardson, L., 92015) Commercial justification for penalty clauses: the death of the old dichotomy. *Edinburgh Law Review,* **19** (1), 119-124.

8 Essential Elements of the Law of Delict

Jill Stirling

Delict is the area of Scots law which deals with legal wrongs. It is sometimes thought to be concerned just with negligence, but the scope of delict is much wider, as will be seen in this and the following two chapters. It is also an area which is still largely dealt with by common law, that is, by cases and courts. This allows a greater degree of flexibility in approach, as what may be defined as a delict can change as society changes. Delicts may be intentional or unintentional (negligence). When one person causes harm to another, there may or may not be liability in delict. The courts are careful to make sure that liability in delict is quite restricted, to make sure that the liability they face if not foreseen is at least foreseeable.

Introduction to the concept of the legal wrong

The Scots law of delict forms part of the law of obligations, along with the law of contract, which together owe their origins to Roman law, as seen in Justinian's Institutes of 533 AD. The English equivalent to delict is tort, but the two legal systems vary in their approach to the problems arising. Scots law takes a general approach which makes it possible to include new delicts as society and circumstances change, whereas English law specifies particular torts, and then faces the problem of having to make new civil wrongs fit the existing categories.

The word delict comes from the Latin *'delictum'* which means 'a legal wrong'. The obligation which the law imposes is to make reparation for the harm done usually by payment of compensation. A delict is a civil wrong, which should not be confused with a crime.

In some circumstances the incident which gives rise to a claim in delict may also constitute a crime. For example, if Adam, while driving his car, knocks Ben down, Ben will have a delict claim against Adam for damages for the injuries he has suffered, but Adam will also be facing prosecution under the Road Traffic legislation for his poor driving. So one incident gives rise to two court appearances for Adam.

It is not always the case that a delict will also be a crime, or that a crime will amount to a delict, and as discussed in Chapter 2 of this book, the standards of proof required in the civil and criminal courts differ. For a finding of liability in a civil delict action, as also with cases in the law of contract and agency, the judge must decide on the *balance of probabilities* that the defender is at fault, whereas in a criminal case the finding of the court that the accused is guilty must be *beyond a reasonable doubt,* which is clearly a harder test.

Like the law of contract, the formal source of most of the law of delict lies in the common law. However, there are certain statutory delicts, some of which will be discussed in Chapter 10.

Not every act that results in harm to a person will give rise to an action in the law of delict. For there to be liability three key elements need to be present.

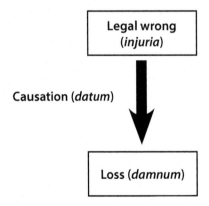

Key concept: *Damnum injuria datum* – loss (harm) must be caused by a legal wrong

These three essential elements will be discussed further in the rest of this chapter.

Intentional v unintentional delicts (negligence)

Delicts can be intentional or unintentional. Intentional delicts include, among others, assault, trespass, fraud, passing off and harassment. Unintentional delicts, where an individual has been negligent, give rise to the concept of the duty of care. It should be emphasised that people are not always liable for the adverse consequences of accidents and other instances where their negligence results in harm to another person. In order for a defender to be made liable for the harm suffered by the pursuer as a result of the defender's negligence, the law poses a number of questions:

1 Was there a duty of care owed by the defender to the pursuer? This is the element of *injuria* referred to in the diagram above.

2 Was this duty breached by some act or omission of the defender which fell below the standard of care of a reasonable person?

3 Did the pursuer suffer a loss? This is the *damnum* (see the diagram).

4 Was it the breach of the defender's duty of care that caused the loss to the pursuer? This is the element referred to as '*datum*' in the diagram.

5 Was it reasonably foreseeable that a loss would occur, or was it too remote to contemplate? The issue of remoteness will be discussed in Chapter 9.

8

> **Tip**
>
> In order for an action for delict to be successful it is necessary for the pursuer to show that the defender is responsible for the wrongful act *and* the damage which has been suffered. The damage must be caused by the wrongful act. If the defender can show that the damage is due to another cause, then the action must fail.

Breach of the duty of care

The case which laid down the general principles of the duty of care was *Donoghue v Stevenson* 1932 S.C. (HL) 31, and in particular the judgment of Lord Atkin. This case, often referred to as 'the snail in the ginger beer,' is regarded as the foundation of modern delict and tort law throughout the common law world. The facts of the case were that Mrs Donoghue and a friend went to a local café, where Mrs D's friend bought her a ginger beer which she poured over ice cream, a concoction known as an ice-cream float.

Ginger beer is traditionally sold in dark brown bottles, which would make it difficult to see if there was anything lurking in the liquid. After consuming some of the ice- cream float, Mrs D poured the remains of the ginger beer over the ice cream. Along with the liquid came a decomposed snail, which Mrs D later claimed had caused her to suffer severe gastro-enteritis, as she had already consumed some of the contaminated drink. The legal problems facing Mrs D were that she had no contract with the manufacturer of the ginger beer, nor did she have a contract with the café owner, since it was her friend who had bought the drink, so she was not in a position to sue either party for the harm caused by that snail. This was the issue at the heart of the case: was it possible to make a manufacturer liable in delict to the consumer of goods, if there was no contractual relationship between them?

While it may seem obvious to us now in an age where consumer protection is accepted as the norm, back in 1932 this was not so clear, which is why the case assumed such importance in the common law world. The case went all the way to the House of Lords, the highest civil court of appeal at the time, where it was held that manufacturers did owe a duty of care to the consumers of their products to ensure that they suffered no harm as a result of any acts or omissions on the part of the manufacturers. This became known as "the neighbour principle" as set out in Lord Atkin's judgment.

Lord Atkin stated in his judgment:

"..Who, then in law is my neighbour? The answer seems to be - persons who are so closely and directly affected by my act that I ought reasonably to have them in contemplation as being so affected when I am directing my mind to the act in question."

The duty of care, and whether or not it exists, is a question of law. It requires consideration of both the ambit of the duty and the reasonable foreseeability that acts, or omissions, of the defender will result in harm to the pursuer. If it is not reasonable to anticipate that there may be harm, as in the case of *Muir v Glasgow Corporation* 1943 S.C. (H.L.) 3, there will be no remedy for the pursuer. The facts of this case were, briefly, that the manageress of a tearoom run by the local council in a park in Glasgow allowed a party of adults and children to take shelter from the rain in the premises, and while there, to get water for making tea. One of the adults, who was carrying an urn full of boiling water, inexplicably let the urn tilt with the result that a girl named Eleanor Muir and some of her friends were scalded. The action for negligence was raised not against the man directly responsible, but the owners of the tearoom, Glasgow Corporation, possibly on the basis that the corporation would have sufficient funds to meet the claim. The case turned on foreseeability; was it reasonably foreseeable that such an incident would happen? The court held that, in the circumstances of this case, it was not.

Similarly, the duty of care has a limited ambit, extending only to those who could reasonably be expected to suffer harm, not to the world in general. The case of *Bourhill v Young* 1942 S.C. (HL) 78 is an example of the limits of the ambit. In this case, Mrs Bourhill had been a passenger on a tram when a motor cyclist crashed into a car, and was killed. Mrs B claimed that the nervous shock she had suffered on hearing the crash had caused her to miscarry her child. It was held that no duty of care could be owed to someone who was not in immediate danger, and who could not have been foreseen as at risk. Had Mrs B been on the road, or pavement, when the collision between the motor cyclist and car happened, then she might well have been in danger; but she was not, and, therefore, her claim failed.

The principle of foreseeability, as laid down by Lord Atkin, has been refined and extended since 1932. Among recent cases looking at this issue, *Caparo Industries plc v Dickman* [1990] 2 A.C. 605 ranks as one of the more important. The facts were that an auditor produced a set of figures which suggested that the financial position of a company was stronger than it was in reality. A number of investors bought shares in the company, basing their decision on the auditor's figures. The shares fell in value, resulting in a loss for the investors. When they tried to claim for this loss, the Court of Appeal held that, despite there being no contractual relationship between the auditor and the investors, the auditor did owe a duty of care to existing shareholders who made further investments, though not to the general public who might decide to purchase shares. However, on appeal, the House of Lords set out three criteria that ALL needed to be fulfilled before a duty of care could be said to exist:

1 the harm suffered by the pursuer must be foreseeable; AND

2 there must be proximity between the pursuer and the defender; AND

3 it must be fair, just and reasonable to impose a duty in the particular circumstances of the case.

This is now known as the 'tripartite test' of duty of care and has been adopted in cases since Caparo.

It was held by the House of Lords that the investors in Caparo failed in their claim on the third part of the test. Auditors prepare accounts for the companies that employ them, not for the general share-buying public, and so do not owe either existing shareholders or new investors a duty of care. The House of Lords held unanimously that to impose such a duty would not be fair, just or reasonable.

This test of what is fair, just and reasonable in the circumstances of each case is in part a matter of public policy, as it allows the court to look at the larger picture, including any possible economic arguments. A good illustration of this is the case of *Hill v Chief Constable of West Yorkshire* [1989] A.C. 53. This case was brought by the mother of the final victim of Peter Sutcliffe, the serial killer known as the Yorkshire Ripper. She sued on the basis that it was negligent of the police to fail to find Sutcliffe, and that it was reasonably foreseeable that he would continue to murder again and again until caught. This case was lost because it failed the second test, that of proximity. Although all of the victims had been women who lived in the Leeds area, it was held that this was too wide a group for there to be a relationship of proximity between them and the police. No duty of care could be said to exist in these circumstances.

A recent case involving another claim of negligence against the police in England is *Rathband v Chief Constable of Northumbria* [2016] E.W.H.C. 181 (QB). The facts of this case were that a known killer, Raoul Moat, had called the police emergency number, 999, to say that he was "hunting for police". Less than nine minutes later, Moat shot PC Rathband as he was sitting in his patrol car, severely injuring and blinding him. Rathband killed himself two years later. The negligence case was brought by Rathband's siblings who claimed that their brother would not have been "a sitting duck" had his police force superiors issued a warning. The judge held that the situation was so fast moving and unprecedented that the police commanders should not be found liable. In the words of Mr Justice Males: "I am acutely conscious that it is easy to be wise after the event and that the dangers of hindsight must be avoided."

As this is a decision at first instance, there might be the possibility of an appeal were it not for the huge costs which the judge awarded against the claimants. Looked at objectively, how long would it have taken the police commanders to broadcast a message of Moat's threat to all forces out in the streets?

Once a duty of care has been established, the next step is to see if the defender has breached the duty. This requires the defender to be acting voluntarily, in other words, to be aware of his actions. Accidents sometimes happen as a result of a driver losing control of his vehicle. The case of *Waugh v James K Allen Ltd* 1943 S.C. (H.L.) 3 is a good example. The facts are as follows: while walking on the pavement of a street in Edinburgh, the pursuer, Mr Waugh, was struck and severely injured by a lorry owned by the defenders and driven by one of their drivers, a Robert Gemmell. The cause of the accident was a heart attack suffered by the driver, who died at the scene. The defenders pleaded that this was an inevitable accident, but the pursuer claimed that, given the state of health of the driver, he, and more importantly his employers, ought to have been aware that he was unfit to drive. The issue put to the court was that the driver, a man of 44 years of age, should have realised that on the day of the accident he was unfit to drive. He had suffered from gastritis on a number of occasions, and the description by his colleagues of the events which immediately preceded the accident, might have led him to believe that he was having yet another attack. Was it reasonable for him to suspect something more sinister? The court held that the pursuer had failed to prove that the driver had acted rashly or negligently.

8

What standard of care is expected?

In most circumstances the law only requires the standard of care of the reasonable man, but this will vary according to the facts of each case. What is a reasonable standard for a bus driver will not be the same as that required of a brain surgeon. There are a number of tests to be applied in determining the risk of harm being caused.

1. What was the likelihood that the defender's acts or omissions would cause harm?

St. George v Home Office [2009] 1 W.L.R. 1670

The facts were as follows: a prisoner was given a top bunk on his arrival to prison, despite explaining that he was addicted to heroin and had suffered from seizures when withdrawing from the drug on previous occasions. He fell from the bunk during a seizure a few nights later and suffered a head injury leading to brain damage. The prison authority was found to be negligent, in part because the risk of placing the claimant in a top bunk had been indicated.

2. How serious was this harm likely to be?

Paris v Stepney Borough Council [1951] A.C. 367

The facts in this case concerned an accident in a garage where a mechanic was struck in the eye by a chip of metal from a car he had been working on. The mechanic was blind in one eye and the metal chip hit his good eye, resulting in total blindness. His employers had not provided him with safety goggles. The standard of care expected of the employers in this case was higher than it would have been with a fully sighted mechanic, because of the severity of the consequences for the plaintiff.

3. Would precautionary measures have been difficult or unduly expensive?

Latimer v A. E. C. Ltd. [1953] A.C. 643

This is another industrial case, this time involving an employee who slipped on a flooded factory floor. He claimed that the factory should have been closed down to avoid such incidents, but the court held that this would have been inconvenient and unnecessary in the circumstances. The employers had spread sawdust on the floor, and this was held by the court to have met the required standard of care.

4. Can the lack of experience of the defender be offered as a defence to a claim in delict?

Nettleship v Weston [1971] 2 Q.B. 691; 3 W.L.R. 370 C.A

The standard of care required by the law is that of the reasonable man. If a defender fails to meet this standard, then he may be found liable. The test is an objective one. The result in the case of *Nettleship* is that a learner driver owes the same standard of care to other road users as an experienced driver. This seems harsh and perhaps unreasonable to anyone who has ever been a learner driver, but it is intended for the protection of other road users and pedestrians, who are entitled to a certain degree of care, not different standards for learners and more experienced drivers.

Has any loss been suffered?

Having established that there was a duty of care which has been breached, the next step is to see if the pursuer has suffered a loss. For example, if our driver Adam is driving too fast, but sees Ben in time to avoid hitting him, there will be no harm done. It is clear that by speeding Adam has breached his duty of care to other road users and pedestrians, but if he does not hit Ben, there is no possible claim in delict.

■ Has the loss been caused by the legal wrong?

As we saw earlier in this chapter, if the pursuer has suffered a loss, it must be demonstrated that this was caused by the defender breaching his duty of care. This causation can be factual, where it is clear that the defender was at fault, or legal, where it is the defender's breach which was the primary cause of the pursuer's loss. For example, if Adam knocks Ben down with his car this will be a matter of fact. Ben is likely to be taken to hospital for his injuries to be treated. If as a result of lying immobile in bed Ben suffers a pulmonary embolism, i.e. a blood clot which moves to the lungs, and dies, can this be attributed to the traffic accident caused by Adam or to substandard treatment in the hospital?

For the defender to be liable in delict, while there will be a factual cause, the breach of duty must be the **legal cause** of the loss.

There are a number of cases which deal with causation, both legal and factual.

McWilliams v Sir William Arrol & Co, Lithgows Ltd 1962 S.C. (H.L) 70

In this case the employers were found to have been in breach of their duty of care by failing to provide a steel erector with a safety belt. They escaped liability when he plunged to his death since it was established in evidence that even if he had been given a belt, he would not have worn it. Provision of the belt would not have stopped the accident, and so the test of causation was not satisfied.

Barnett v Chelsea and Kensington Hospital Management Committee [1969] 1 Q.B. 428

A man presented to the emergency department of the hospital complaining of sickness and vomiting. Instead of being seen by a doctor, the man was sent home and died later that night. This would look like a clear breach of the hospital's duty of care. However, the evidence established that the man had been poisoned with arsenic, and there would have been nothing that any doctor could have done to help him. His death was inevitable. Breach of duty could not be said to be the legal cause of his death; the cause of death was arsenic poisoning.

It is possible for the chain of causation linking the defender's breach of duty to the pursuer's loss to be broken; this could be by something done by third parties, or even by the pursuer. This break is referred to as a *novus*

8

actus interveniens, or a new act intervening, which will be discussed in the next chapter. In the example above of Ben and his death following the traffic accident, could it be argued that it was the poor medical care which broke the chain of causation?

McKew v Holland and Hannen and Cubitts (Scotland) Ltd 1970 S.C. (H.L.) 20

The pursuer in this case had injured his ankle as a result of the defender's negligence. The result was a weakness in the joint, rendering his leg liable to give way. Shortly after this first incident, the pursuer was going down a steep staircase which lacked a handrail. His leg gave way, and he panicked. Instead of continuing to descend as best he could, he jumped down 10 steps, injuring his leg further. Although the first event led on to the second, it was not the primary cause of the injuries suffered in the second incident. The actions of the pursuer in jumping down the steps constituted a *novus actus interveniens*. The pursuer was responsible for his second injury.

■ *Res ipsa loquitur* and the reversal of the burden of proof

In some circumstances the pursuer who has suffered the loss may have no idea how it came about. Typically these cases involve loads being dropped on the pursuer, often by cranes either being incorrectly operated or having some defect in their mechanisms. Where the pursuer has clearly suffered harm, the courts will tend to infer from the facts that there must have been some sort of negligence otherwise the incident could not have happened. This is important because it might otherwise be impossible for the pursuer to obtain the necessary evidence that there has been negligence. These cases are given the Latin tag *res ipsa loquitur* which translates as "the thing speaks for itself". There are two requirements which must be satisfied:

1 The nature of the incident could only have occurred if there has been some carelessness on the part of the defender; AND

2 The thing which caused the accident was within the exclusive control of the defender.

If the pursuer is able to show these two requirements, the normal burden of proof, that is, the need for the pursuer to prove that it was the defender who caused the harm, is reversed, and the defender is deemed to have been negligent. The defender is only able to escape liability, if he can provide an alternative explanation for the incident which has caused the harm.

The case of *Scott v London and St Katherine Docks Co* [1861-73] All E.R. Rep 248 is a good example of the crane dropping its load cases, where the plaintiff was successful, whereas *Easson v London & North East Railway* [1944] K.B. 421 is an example of a case where the defendant was able to provide an alternative explanation for the incident, and, therefore, escaped liability.

A Scottish case which referenced Scott is *Devine v Colvilles Ltd* 1969 S.C. (HL) 67. The pursuer was injured when he jumped from a platform about 15 feet above ground at the Ravenscraig steel works. There had been a violent explosion some 75 yards away and the pursuer feared for his safety. The only basis for the pursuer's case was *res ipsa loquitur*. The defenders failed to prove that they had taken all steps to inspect the oxygen hoses which had burst, causing the incident, and were, therefore liable to the pursuer.

Exercise

Fred, a hotel chef, was involved in fighting a fire in the hotel kitchen, which was caused by lack of maintenance by the hotel. While he was not physically injured, after the fire a pre-existing skin-condition flared up, and Fred now wants to sue the hotel for negligence, in relation to his skin condition. However, the hotel management is of the view that this is coincidental and nothing to do with the fire.

8

Referring to the three essential requirements that must be present for there to be liability in negligence, which one or more may be missing here?

Conclusion

This chapter explored the elements that must be proved if a person is to be liable for involuntarily causing harm to another person: there must be a loss caused by a legal wrong. Delicts can either be intentional or the result of negligence. For a person to be liable in negligence, they must owe a duty of care, which has been breached. The law takes quite a narrow approach, as it is not desirable to make defenders potentially liable to indeterminate large numbers of people. Therefore the harm must be reasonably foreseeable, and the parties in a relationship of proximity. The chapter also considers the circumstances where the causal link is missing, and the consequences would have arisen even if the defender had taken reasonable care: in these cases there is no liability in delict.

Further reading

Black, G., (editor), (2015) *Business Law in Scotland*, 3rd edition Edinburgh: W. Green Chapter 10.

Cameron,G., (2011) *Law Basics: Delict*, 4th edition Edinburgh: W. Green. Chapters 1 and 2.

McManus, F., and Russell, E. (2011) *Delict: a Comprehensive Guide to the Law* 2nd edition, Dundee: Dundee University Press. Chapters 1, 2, 6 and 7.

McManus, F., (2013) *Delict Essentials* 2nd edition Edinburgh: Edinburgh University Press. Chapter 1 and Chapter 2.

Stewart,W.J., (2004) *Delict* 4th edition Edinburgh: W. Green, Chapters 1 and 9.

Thomson,J., (2014) *Delictual Liability*, 5th edition Edinburgh: Bloomsbury Professional. Chapters 1-6.

9 Particular Issues Concerning the Duty of Care

Jill Stirling

In Chapter 8 the concept of a duty of care was introduced through the case of *Donoghue v Stevenson*. This case highlighted the importance in the Scots law of delict, and the English law of tort, of the duty owed to our neighbours to use reasonable care. This chapter deals with the different types of situations where this duty is to be found, and also the circumstances where there is no duty, and therefore, no claim in delict.

Pure omissions

In Scots Law there is no general legal duty to warn someone of a potential danger, or to rescue that person from harm. In other jurisdictions, such as New York state, in the USA, there may be a possible prosecution under criminal law for 'depraved indifference' if a person fails to act in a situation where it is clear that serious harm will be suffered by a victim.

There are exceptions to these general rules:

1 Where there is a sufficiently close degree of proximity, between the parties; **or**

2 Where it is the person who is creating the danger who fails to warn the victim.

Nervous shock

The duty to cause no harm through negligence is not limited to physical harm, but also covers situations where the pursuer is suffering from mental health problems as a result of the delictual event. However, the courts have put strict limits on the situations where a duty of care can be said to exist to prevent nervous shock, despite the advances in the medical recognition of the effects of Post-Traumatic Stress over the past one hundred years.

If the pursuer who is suffering from nervous shock was also at risk of physical harm as a result of the defender's carelessness, the claim may succeed.

If the pursuer in this situation was not at risk of physical harm in circumstances where someone else was injured due to the defender's negligence the claim will only succeed, if the following three tests can be satisfied:

1 There were 'close ties of affection' between the pursuer and the actual victim; **and**

2 The pursuer witnessed the incident or its immediate aftermath; **and**

3 The pursuer saw or heard the effects of the incident on the victim.

The three leading cases on nervous shock all arose from disasters which would, in all likelihood, have resulted in ongoing mental health issues for the pursuers/claimants, yet none of them succeeded in satisfying the three tests. They are:

Alcock and Others v Chief Constable of South Yorkshire [1991] 4 All E.R. 907 (H.L.)

This case arose out of the tragedy at the Sheffield Wednesday football ground in April 1989, when the police allowed late arrivals to enter a part of the stadium that was already full, with the result that 96 Liverpool fans at the front were pushed into the security fencing and crushed to death. The match was being televised live and many of the claimants who sought damages had seen the event on TV. Because they had not been present at the event, their claims failed.

Robertson v Forth Road Bridge Joint Board 1994 S.L.T. 56

This claim failed the close ties of affection test. *Alcock* had decided that those who qualified for this test should not be limited to parents and children and husbands and wives, but could include fiancees. The court did not extend the class of potential claimants to a brother or brother-in-law, so it was not surprising that the court in *Robertson* did not allow a claim by a workmate, even one of twenty years' close friendship with the victim.

McFarlane v E. E. Caledonia Ltd [1994] 2 All E.R. 1

This case arose out of the explosion of the Piper Alpha oil rig in the North Sea. The pursuer was on a supply vessel some distance from the rig when it exploded killing 167 workers. This claim also failed the close ties of affection test.

Economic loss

If the pursuer's case is based on the loss of money alone, no matter that the sum may be large, the courts will not usually allow the claim. A possible reason for this is that the loss may have been insurable. In these circumstances the courts will not allow a legal claim, where there is already a practical solution. Another possible reason is that it would give rise to too much potential liability. A good example of this is this English case:

Spartan Steel & Alloys Ltd v Martin & Co (Contractors) Ltd [1973] 1 Q.B. 27; [1972] 3 All E.R. 557.

The claimants had a stainless steel factory in Birmingham, England. Its electricity supply came directly from the power station. The defendants were doing work outside the factory with an excavator and negligently damaged the cable. The cable was the property of the power company. As a consequence of the defendants' negligence, the factory was without power for 15 hours. This resulted in:

1 physical damage to the factory's furnaces and metal;

2 lost profit on the damaged metal; and

3 lost profit on the metal that was not processed during the time the power was off.

The claimants claimed for all three heads of damage and succeeded under heads (1) and (2), but not under head (3). The reasoning of the court was that head (1) related to physical damage and head (2) was directly consequential on head (1), but the profits lost during the outage were "pure economic loss", in other words, only money. There was an acceptance by the court that the defendants did owe a duty of care to the claimants, and the damage was not too remote, since it was foreseeable. The rejection of the claim for pure economic loss was for policy reasons, including the "floodgates argument," as outlined by Lord Denning MR in his leading judgment.

Pursuers are able to claim for economic loss that results from physical harm: for example if Claire is injured as a result of Dan's negligence, and Claire is unable to work for a period of time with resultant loss of wages, she can claim damages for the loss of that income.

There are exceptions to the general prohibition against obtaining a remedy for pure economic loss.

■ Economic loss arising from negligent misstatements

There may be a duty of care not to cause pure economic loss through giving negligent advice or information if

1 The person giving the advice knew that it would be relied on by the other party, **and**

2 The person giving the advice knew or should have known that it would be used by the other party in a particular transaction or a particular kind of transaction.

The leading cases are:

Hedley Byrne & Co v Heller & Partners [1964] A.C. 465; [1963] 3 W.L.R. 101, (H.L.)

The House of Lords held in this case that a duty of care could be owed when a reference was given in relation to a banker's client, even if the loss was purely financial. The party relying on the reference incurred substantial costs on behalf of the client, which went unpaid. This was foreseeable and should have entitled the plaintiffs to damages, but the claim was lost because the bankers had included a disclaimer of liability in the letter they had provided.

Martin v Bell-Ingram 1986 S.L.T. 575

This case arose from the provision of a negligent survey to purchasers of a house. Although technically the survey was required by the providers of the finance to the house purchasers, it was commonly understood that it would be used by the purchasers in making their decision to buy the property, and they would be paying for it. Before **Martin,** surveyors had escaped liability on the basis that their duty of care was owed to the lender, not the borrower.

Caparo Industries v Dickman [1990] 2 W.L.R. 358

This case was discussed in Chapter 8.

■ Economic loss arising from defective products and services

There is normally now no duty of care in respect of pure economic loss caused by defective products and services. This has not always been the case. In the early 1970s the courts were increasingly sympathetic to such claims, but more recent cases have swung back to the previous, less generous, position. This may be for public policy reasons, particularly where the cost of meeting such claims would fall on public bodies, such as local authorities.

Recent cases are:

D & F Estates v Church Commissioners for England [1988] 3 W.L.R. 368

This case arose from the construction of a block of flats between 1963 and 1965 on land owned by the defendants. Plasterwork was carried out by subcontractors for the defendants, who subsequently leased a flat to the claimants. Some 15 years later, the plasterwork was found to be defective, and some of it fell off. Remedial work was carried out by the claimants, and it was the cost of this, plus associated expenses, which was being claimed. The House of Lords determined that this was another example of pure economic loss which was not recoverable.

Murphy v Brentwood District Council [1990] 3 W.L.R. 414

The council issued a completion certificate in respect of foundations for a property. The foundations were later found to be defective and the property became unstable. The owner could not afford to remedy the defects and consequently suffered a considerable loss on resale of the property; he claimed the difference from the District Council. The House of Lords, again, found this to be pure economic loss, and, in the absence of any physical injury associated with the defects, rejected the claim. It is likely that public policy, the 'floodgates argument' in particular, played a large part in this decision.

The case is significant because it overruled an earlier decision of the House of Lords in *Anns v Merton London Borough Council* [1978] A.C. 728.

9

Remoteness of loss

A pursuer will be unsuccessful in a claim for damage if the courts consider that the harm was too remote. There are two possible tests to be applied:

1 Once liability is established, the defender is liable for all losses that flow naturally and directly from the negligence. This is similar to what would happen with a claim under contract.

 This test tends to be applied by the Scottish courts.

2 Alternatively, once liability is established, the defender is only liable for those losses which are reasonably foreseeable.

 This is the test usually applied by the English courts.

In most cases the result is the same, whichever test is used.

A case which is a good illustration of remoteness of loss is *Overseas Tankship (UK) Ltd v Mort Docks & Engineering Co (The Wagon Mound No 1)* [1961] A.C. 388.

This was an appeal to the Privy Council from the Australian Courts, in which the English test was applied.

The facts were as follows: heavy furnace oil, a type of oil which does not burn easily, was negligently spilt from a ship in Sydney harbour. Workmen using welding equipment were working on the wharf. Molten metal from the welding fell into the harbour. This ignited cotton waste floating on the oil, and set the oil ablaze. The fire which ensued destroyed the wharf and some adjacent buildings.

The Privy Council decided that, in order to be recoverable, the damage had to be a reasonably foreseeable consequence of the original negligent spillage. Given the low combustibility of the oil, the defenders could not have foreseen that the result would be an enormous fire. They were found not liable.

A recent Scottish case in this area is *Simmons v British Steel* 2004 S.C. (HL) 94.

This case arose from an accident at the pursuer's workplace, Clyde Bridge Steel Works, which left him with physical and psychiatric injuries, some of which appeared several weeks after the initial event. The issue of remoteness was dealt with at length by their lordships, but their judgments show an acceptance of the causal connection between the physical injuries suffered at the outset and the psychiatric injuries which appeared later. The House of Lords held that as British Steel was liable for the physical injuries incurred in the accident, as there was sufficient causal connection, it was liable for the consequent additional physical and psychiatric problems that arose later: as Simmons was a primary victim, there was no need to prove that the additional injuries were reasonably foreseeable.

The law applies 'the Thin Skull Rule' in circumstances where the defender has caused more harm to the pursuer than might ordinarily have been anticipated. The rule lays down that the defender must take his victim as he finds him. If the defender knocks someone down with a single blow and this results in serious injury or possibly death, because of the victim's physical state, such as a thinner than normal skull, the defender cannot claim that such an outcome was not reasonably foreseeable and is, therefore, too remote. *Simmons v British Steel* is an example of this concept.

McKillen v Barclay Curle & Co Ltd 1967 S.L.T. 41.

The facts of this case are quite simple. The pursuer had suffered from tuberculosis. An accident at work which resulted in a fractured rib reactivated the TB. The defenders were liable to the pursuer not just for the negligence which had caused his fractured rib, but also for the recurrence of the TB.

As seen in Chapter 8, events may intervene which break the chain of causation (*novus actus interveniens*).

9

Exercise

Bill was slightly injured in a road traffic accident caused by the negligence of Mary. While lying on the pavement, waiting for an ambulance, John drove round the corner at speed and injured Bill much more severely.

Would Mary be liable for the additional injuries suffered by Bill, or do John's acts break the chain of causation?

Prescription and limitation of actions

There are limits to the length of time you can wait before raising a claim in delict. 'Prescription' refers to the extinction of obligations after a period of time, though not all delictual obligations prescribe. 'Limitation of actions' refers to the fact that certain claims become unenforceable if they are not raised within a certain time. The law is governed by the Prescription and Limitation (Scotland) Act 1973.

■ Limitation of actions

The law imposes time limits for bringing legal actions. This is practical, as memory of the events will fade over time. If a pursuer wishes to bring an action in delict for personal injuries or death caused by negligence, the writ must be issued before the expiry of three years from the date of the accident, otherwise the claim is unenforceable. If the action is for compensation for health problems, which have arisen as a result of exposure to a toxic substance such as asbestos, which can lead to the fatal lung condition mesothelioma, the three year period starts to run from the date the pursuer was first made aware of the condition. If this were not possible, the time limits would have expired years before the pursuer was even aware of any fatal condition.

■ Prescription

Most actions for delict prescribe if there has not been a claim or acknowledgement of the existence of the obligation within five years from the date on which the loss or damage occurred, or the date on which the pursuer became aware of the loss injury or damage. (It is six years under English law for actions in tort.) Some claims are imprescriptable, including claims for personal injuries and death. Some claims prescribe only after 20 years, such as claims based on defamation. Claims based on product liability prescribe after ten years, as set out in the Consumer Protection Act 1987 (Chapter 10).

The courts tend to apply these time limits quite strictly; although in rare situations it may be possible for the pursuer to bring an action beyond the three or five year limits, with the express permission of the courts, where it is just and equitable to do so. If there were no such limits, defenders could face years of uncertainty, not knowing if their victims might bring a legal action against them.

Defences to an action for negligence

There are six defences available:

■ Statutory authority

Parliament may pass legislation authorising an activity which might other-wise give rise to an action in negligence. If this defence is being used, the relevant statute must be examined to determine the extent of this authority.

A case which illustrates this is *Vaughan v Taff Vale Railway* (1860) 5 H. & N. 679.

The construction of a railway was authorised by statute, as was required in the 19th Century. Despite every precaution being taken, sparks from the train engine escaped and set fire to the verge beside the track. It was held that the statutory authority for the building of the railway included an implied right to use the land surrounding the line, and this was an acceptable defence to the action.

A contrasting case is *Managers of the Metropolitan Asylum District v Hill* (1881) 6 App. Cas. 193.

The facts of this were that a statute, the Metropolitan Poor Act 1867, allowed for the building of hospitals "of such nature and size. . . as [they] think fit." An infectious diseases hospital was built near the plaintiff's house. He brought an action for nuisance, on the ground that the hospital posed a risk of infection from smallpox. The defence of statutory authority was offered, but it failed. The court held that the local authority had no authority to locate the hospital where it would constitute a nuisance, such as in a residential area.

If damage occurs as a result, it is still possible that an action could be raised, if the authorised activity could have been carried out without causing damage.

■ Necessity

This may be a valid defence if a wrongful act is done for a good reason. For example, if it is necessary to break down a door, a delict, in order to rescue someone from a burning building, the greater good of saving a life outweighs the damage to the door.

■ Damnum fatale

This is also known as 'inevitable accident' or 'act of God' and can only be used where there has been an unexpected and purely natural event, which could not have been foreseen. The sort of event covered by this defence would be damage caused by a tropical storm, earthquake, tsunami, or eruption of a volcano. If the damage has been made worse by human activity, or inactivity, it cannot be claimed as a *damnum fatale.*

An example of devastation which was originally thought to be an act of God would be the flooding of large areas of the American city of New Orleans, after it was hit by Hurricane Katrina in 2005. The initial damage caused by the strong winds and rain could be attributed to the hurricane. However, the flooding, which occurred three days after the storm, when the levees protecting the city from the Mississippi River and Lake Pontchartrain burst, was later found to be the result of inadequate engineering. Furthermore, computer studies into the likelihood of the city flooding in the event of a direct hit by a hurricane of the same strength as Katrina had been carried out a few years earlier. These studies had shown exactly the same locations for breaches of the levees as occurred when the storm hit. The damage caused by Hurricane Katrina, therefore, fails the tests for act of God in that it had been foreseen and was largely due to human failings. By contrast, the tsunami which caused such major loss of life around the Indian Ocean on 26th December 2004 was the result of an undersea earthquake which could not have been foreseen, and was, therefore, a true *damnum fatale.*

There is an old Scottish case which concerns liability for flood damage which resulted from interference with a natural watercourse.

Caledonian Railway Co v Greenock Corporation 1917 S.C. (HL) 56.

The facts of this case were that the defenders had altered the channel of a stream and enclosed it in a culvert in order to improve the amenity of a public park. Following heavy rainfall the stream flooded, causing damage to the pursuers' property. The defenders attempted to use the defence of *damnum fatale,* but the court held that heavy rainfall, even exceptionally heavy rainfall, was hardly an uncommon event in Scotland and so the defence failed.

■ Volenti non fit injuria

If a pursuer voluntarily assumes the risk of injury, which results in the harm being claimed for, the defender can use this as a defence. If it is proved, this defence ends the pursuer's legal action for compensation, but for this reason, the courts tend to construe it narrowly. The defender must show that the pursuer was fully aware of the risk and freely consented to the activity which led to the harm. This consent can be either express or implied.

The English case of *Morris v Murray* [1990] 3 All E.R.801 is an excellent example of the defence succeeding. The plaintiff and M got into M's light aircraft after both had been drinking heavily. The weather was poor, and no other planes were flying, yet the pair got into the aircraft and proceeded to take off. The plane crashed almost immediately, killing the pilot and seriously injuring the plaintiff. The Court of Appeal held that any claim in negligence was defeated by the defence of *volenti*.

The defence is unlikely to succeed in two situations:

1   Where the person who undertakes the risk does so to save life or rescue property, the court will seldom regard such a person as *volenti*, if he is injured.

   An example of this situation can be found in the case of *Baker v T E Hopkins & Sons Ltd* [1959] 1 W.L.R. 966;[1959] 3 All E.R. 225, in which a doctor climbed down a well to treat two workers who had been overcome by fumes. The doctor was aware of the dangerous fumes. The court held that his act in going down the well was not *volenti*, and the doctor was in the class of persons that the defendants should have reasonably anticipated as likely to go to the assistance of injured employees, and hence the defendants were liable for negligence in relation to the doctor's death.

2   Where an employer tries to use it to escape liability to an injured employee.

The use of the *volenti* defence is also restricted by legislation:

Road Traffic Act 1988 s.149

The defence does not apply in an action brought by a passenger against the d river of a vehicle with compulsory third party insurance.

Consumer Rights Act 2015 s.62 and s.65

These sections apply to non-contractual notices as well as contract terms. A notice which tries to exclude liability for breach of duty (including a duty of care) will be void where it relates to death or personal injury, and unenforceable in other cases unless it is fair and reasonable.

Contributory negligence

It is a defence to show that the pursuer's loss and injury was partly due to his own fault.

Law Reform (Contributory Negligence) Act 1945 s.1 (1)

In order to succeed, the defender must show that the pursuer's conduct fell below the standard of a reasonable person in his position, and that the conduct was the factual cause of the damage.

A common situation where this defence is likely to be successful would be a road traffic accident. Although occupants of cars are now required by law to wear seat belts, unless they have been granted an exemption, there will still be people who refuse to buckle up. Should that person be injured in a crash caused by the driver, and subsequently make a claim for damages against either the driver, or more usually, the driver's insurer, it will be a valid defence to state that the pursuer contributed to his own injuries by failing to wear a seat belt.

The consequence of this defence is a reduction in the amount of damages awarded equivalent to the amount of contribution made by the pursuer's actions.

■ Criminality

For public policy reasons, the courts will not award damages where one person harmed another when the pursuer, or both parties were engaged in some criminal activity. For example, if the pursuer is injured when a car crashes, being driven at excessive speed by the defender, there will be no award of damages, if it can be shown that the pursuer was encouraging the defender to exceed the speed limit.

An English case which illustrates this well is *Pitts v Hunt* [1991] 1Q.B. 24

The plaintiff was riding on the back of a motorcycle which was being driven recklessly when it was in collision with a car. Evidence showed that the plaintiff had been encouraging the driver to ride recklessly, and to intimidate other road users. His claim for damages was rejected on the grounds that he had been involved in an illegal activity.

Remedies

There are two basic remedies for delict:

■ Interdict (= Injunction in English law)

If the wrong is a continuing one, the pursuer will want it to be stopped. If the pursuer anticipates that a future wrong is intended to be committed by the defender, and there are reasonable grounds for believing this to be so, the pursuer can apply for an interdict to stop the defender.

■ Damages

The purpose of financial compensation is to restore the pursuer, as far as possible, to the position he was in before the delict happened. This is known as '*restitutio in integrum*'.

In the case of an action for personal injuries, or death, the award of damages is divided into distinct categories:

(1) Patrimonial Loss

This includes:

- ☐ loss of wages to the date of the proof (trial), together with a calculation for future loss, if the injuries are ongoing;
- ☐ the cost of any medical expenses arising from the accident;
- ☐ interest on both of these sums at varying rates.

Various deductions may be made from this head of damages, such as income tax and the recovery of any state benefits the pursuer may have received,

(2) Solatium

The pursuer is entitled to claim for:

- ☐ pain and suffering; and
- ☐ loss of faculties, for example, loss of vision, limbs etc.; and
- ☐ shortened expectation of life, per s.1 of the Damages (Scotland) Act 2011.

Conclusion

Whereas Chapter 8 set out the basic requirements for a valid case in delict, Chapter 9 focused on and developed particular issues of difficulty where the courts have drawn some boundaries to what they will allow, sometimes resulting in seemingly unjust outcomes. These seemingly harsh decisions may be made for reasons of public policy, because even more undesirable consequences of excessively wide liability that might follow if the court accepted there was liability in some of these hard cases. It is unhelpful to discuss these cases in terms of 'fairness.' The chapter also discussed the possible defences that might be used, and the remedies available to the pursuer in an action for delict.

Further reading

Black, G., (editor), (2015) *Business Law in Scotland*, 3rd edition Edinburgh: W. Green Chapter 10.

Cameron, G., (2011) *Law Basics: Delict*, 4th edition Edinburgh: W. Green, Chapters 3, 4 and 10.

McManus, F. and Russell, E., (2011) *Delict: a Comprehensive Guide to the Law* 2nd edition, Dundee: Dundee University Press, Chapters 3-5, 7 -10, 21 and 22.

McManus, F., (2013) *Delict Essentials* 2nd edition Edinburgh: Edinburgh University Press, Chapter 2,10 and 11.

Stewart,WJ., (2004) *Delict* 4th edition Edinburgh: W. Green, Chapters 10,11 25 & 26.

Thomson,J., (2014) *Delictual Liability*, 5th edition Edinburgh: Bloomsbury Professional, Chapters 4, 5, 6 and 16.

10 **Particular Delicts**

Jill Stirling

We have now explored the legal rules that determine when a person can and cannot raise an action in the law of delict. Some delicts have names (nominate delicts), and these are the subject of this chapter. In many respects they follow the same rules as have already been discussed in the last two chapters.

Professional negligence

A professional person must attain the standard of care which would be expected of a reasonably competent member of his profession. This means that the standard will be higher than that expected of the ordinary man. If the professional person does not have the expected level of expertise or experience, yet gives the impression to the world that he does, he will be held to that higher standard in the event of an action for negligence being raised against him.

In order for a pursuer to succeed in an action for professional negligence he must show three things:

1 There was a normal practice for the profession; AND

2 The defender did not follow the normal practice; AND

3 The course followed by the defender would not have been followed by any other member of the profession of ordinary skill, acting with ordinary care.

The case of *Hunter v Hanley* 1955 S.C. 200 laid down these tests.

The facts of the case were as follows: the defender was giving the pursuer the 12th of a series of injections of penicillin when the hypodermic needle snapped, causing injury to the pursuer. It was the pursuer's contention that the type of needle used was not strong enough, and that "any doctor possessing a fair and average knowledge of his profession would have known this."

In order to succeed, the pursuer must establish all three parts; failure to prove any one dooms the case.

Liability for the delicts of others

The normal rule is that a person is liable for his own delicts and cannot usually be made liable for the delicts of others. There are exceptions:

■ Joint and several liability

This will arise where two or more people are responsible for the same delict (joint wrongdoers). In this situation, the pursuer can choose which of several defenders to sue, or the pursuer can sue them all. The court can apportion damages between the parties, according to liability, and defenders who have been successfully sued may be able to recover damages from the others. This statutory rule is found in s.3 of the Law Reform (Miscellaneous Provisions) (Scotland) Act 1940.

■ Vicarious liability

In some, limited, circumstances, when one person commits a delict, liability can be imposed on someone who was not involved and is, therefore, not at fault. The actual perpetrator is jointly and severally liable with the person who is vicariously liable. (Vicarious means in place of another.) There are some public policy justifications for vicarious liability, as will be seen. While the party who is found liable vicariously for the delict of another person can pursue a remedy against that person, generally this does not happen, as often a claim can be made on insurance.

It is important to note that parents are not vicariously liable for the delicts of their children, but may be found to have exercised insufficient control over them, resulting in harm to others, and this can give rise to legal claims in the law of delict against the parents, whose liability is direct and not vicarious.

There are three relationships where vicarious liability may arise:

Principal and agent

As will be seen in Chapter 11, an agency relationship comes into being where one person is authorised to act for another. A principal will be vicariously liable for the delicts of his agent where he expressly authorised the act in question, or where the agent was acting within the scope of his implied authority. If the delict happens in neither of these situations, the agent will be personally liable.

Independent contractors

The general rule is that a person is *not* vicariously liable for the actions of an independent contractor he has hired. However, if the person engaging the independent contractor has full control of what the contractor does, and how he does it, then that 'employer' may incur vicarious liability, and the case law suggests that a person who commissions work from an independent contractor may have vicarious liability, if the work involves extra-hazardous acts.

Employers and employees

Employers are generally liable for the delicts of their employees, if the pursuer can establish two things:

1 The relationship between the person who committed the delict and the defender is genuinely that of employer and employee. In some situations it may not be clear if the wrongdoer is an employee or an independent contractor, and the courts will apply an objective test to determine the reality. The names the parties use to describe their relationship are not conclusive. If an employee has been seconded to another employer on a temporary basis, the original employer will remain vicariously liable, unless it can be shown that full control of the employee has passed to the new employer.

2 The delict was committed during the course of the employee's employment. The words 'course of employment' can be widely interpreted. The employee will be acting in the course of his employment if he doing work he is authorised to do, even if he is doing it in an unauthorised or prohibited way. A case which illustrates this is *Rose v Plenty* [1976] 1 All E.R. 97.

10

The facts were as follows: A milkman hired a 13 year old boy to help him with his deliveries. This was in flagrant breach of his employer's policy. The boy was injured when the milkman drove the milk float negligently. The dairy was found vicariously liable as the boy's presence on the float was in pursuance of the employer's business.

If the employee is doing something which is clearly beyond the boundaries of his employment, then the employer will not be liable.

Several cases illustrate this:

Raynor v Mitchell (1877) L.R. 2 CPD 257

The facts of this case are as follows: A brewery worker who took his employer's van without permission and used it for private purposes was not acting within the scope of his employment, even though he picked up some empty barrels on his way to return the van. His employers were not liable for injuries he caused when driving the van.

Poland v John Parr & Sons [1927] 1 K.B. 236

The facts of this case may seem bizarre! A van driver who assaulted a boy he thought was stealing from his employer's van was held to be acting within the scope of his employment, because he was acting to protect his employer's property. As a result, the employer was vicariously liable for the assault.

Warren v Henly's [1958] 2 All E.R. 935

Another bizarre set of facts! A customer at a petrol station was abused by the attendant as he drove off without paying. The customer returned to the petrol station and paid for his fuel. He then called the police and threatened to report the attendant to his employers. At that point the attendant physically assaulted the customer, who now sued the employer. Held: The employers were not liable. The act of assault was one of personal revenge, and was outside the scope of his employment.

A recent English case extended the vicarious liability of employers in relation to sexual offences committed against young care home residents.

Lister v Hesley Hall Ltd [2002] 1 A.C. 215

A boarding house in Doncaster was opened in 1979 for students aged 12 to 15 with behavioural and emotional difficulties. The house was run by a warden, who lived there with his disabled wife. It had been alleged by some of the boys that the warden had sexually abused them, including gifting them unwarranted surprises, and taking trips alone with them. A criminal investigation took place some ten years later, resulting in the warden being sentenced to seven years imprisonment; following this, the victims brought an action for personal injury against the employers, alleging they were vicariously liable. The leading judgment is by Lord Steyn:

> "I am satisfied that in the case of the appeals under consideration the evidence showed that the employers entrusted the care of the children . . . to the warden. The question is whether the warden's torts were so closely connected with his employment that it would be fair and just to hold the employers vicariously liable. On the facts of the case the answer is yes. After all, the sexual abuse was inextricably interwoven with the carrying out by the warden of his duties. Matters of degree arise. But the present cases clearly fall on the side of vicarious liability."

More abuse of a customer can be found in the 2016 case of *Mohamud v Wm Morrison Supermarkets plc* [2016] 2 W.L.R. 821, a case decided by the Supreme Court. When Mr Mohamud was violently assaulted by a petrol pump assistant employed by Morrisons, he argued that the supermarket should be vicariously liable for his attacker's actions. The claim failed at trial and before the Court of Appeal. The Supreme Court had to consider how the law in this area has developed and whether it was in need of significant change.

Mohamud v Wm Morrison Supermarkets plc **[2016] 2 W.L.R. 821**

The facts of the case:

Mr Mohamud went to a Morrisons' petrol station in Birmingham. He asked whether the garage could print off some images from a USB stick.

Amjid Khan worked behind the counter. He responded to Mr Mohamud's request with foul and abusive language. Mr Mohamud protested at being spoken to in this manner, which led to another barrage of abuse from Mr Khan, who ordered Mr Mohamud to leave.

Mr Mohamud went to his car, but was followed by Mr Khan. Mr Khan opened the passenger door and told him in a threatening manner never to come back. When Mr Mohamud asked him to shut the door, he was punched by Mr Khan. Mr Mohamud got out of the car to close the passenger door. Mr Khan punched him to the ground and severely assaulted him, despite his supervisor telling him to stop.

10

At trial and appeal it had been held that Morrisons were not vicariously liable for Mr Khan's actions. Although his job involved some interaction with customers, it involved nothing more than serving and helping them. There was not a sufficiently close connection between what he was employed to do and assaulting a customer.

Mr Mohamud had died before the case went to the Supreme Court, but his family continued with the action and argued that the test of 'close connection' was outdated. They sought a new, broader test of 'representative capacity': was Mr Khan acting in the capacity of a representative of the employer at the time of the assault? Alternatively, was Mr Khan was acting within the 'field of activities' assigned to him in dealing with Mr Mohamud?

The decision

The Supreme Court allowed the appeal, holding Morrisons vicariously liable for Mr Khan's actions. They considered the development of vicarious liability. The test for many years was whether the employee's conduct was "either (a) a wrongful act authorised by the master or (b) a wrongful and unauthorised mode of doing some act authorised by the master."

However, in *Lister v Hesley Hall Ltd*, above, the court recognised that the second leg of this test was ineffective. It introduced the 'close connection' test to remedy this.

The court saw no need to alter the test in the way proposed by Mr Mohamud. The close connection test was sufficient. Mr Khan's job was to attend to customers and respond to their inquiries. His foul-mouthed response and ordering Mr Mohamud to leave was inexcusable but within the 'field of activities' assigned to him. There was no break in the chain by Mr Khan then following Mr Mohamud to his car. In Lord Toulson's view, "It was a seamless episode." Further, when he opened the passenger door, he ordered Mr Mohamud to keep away from his employer's premises, which was reinforced by the assault. It was not something personal between them.

The fact that it was a gross abuse of his position was irrelevant, as was Mr Khan's true motive. Morrisons had entrusted him to deal with members of the public and it was just that they should be responsible for his abuse of this trust.

There ar e public policy reasons why employers should be vicariously liable for the acts of their employees: firstly, the employer set up the system of work in which the accident occurred and secondly by the Employers' Liability (Compulsory Insurance) Act 1969, employers must hold insurance for the acts of their employees.

Normally people are liable for their own delicts. Why should certain people be liable vicariously for the delicts of others? Are the boundaries clearly enough drawn?

Employer's liability for employees

■ Common Law

An employer has a duty at common law to take reasonable care for the safety of his employees, and this is an implied term in every contract of employment. The duty is personal to the employer and cannot be delegated to someone else. There are three elements to this duty:

1 A duty to provide proper plant and equipment: this covers initial provision and maintenance.

2 A duty to provide reasonably competent fellow workers: this also covers independent contractors used by the employer.

3 A duty to provide a safe system of work: this covers safe work methods and compliance, as well as the provision of safety equipment.

English v Wilsons and Clyde Coal Co. 1937 S.C. (H.L.) 46

This case combined breach of the common law duty of care and statutory breach of s.74 of the Coal Mines Act of 1911.

■ Statutory Duty

There are many statutes which create liabilities which go beyond the common law, but the main protections for workers are to be found in the Health and Safety at Work Act 1974. The act provides criminal penalties for breaches, but its subsidiary Regulations provide the possibility of civil remedies. There are a further six sets of Regulations, which owe their origins to EU Directives, and of these five allow for civil actions against employers.

10

Occupiers' liability

The occupier of property owes a duty of reasonable care to anyone who enters the property. At common law the standard of care depended on the status of the person entering the property: whether this was an invitee or a trespasser. If the latter, no duty of care was owed. This was changed in the Occupiers' Liability (Scotland) Act 1960.

Under the Occupiers' Liability (Scotland) Act 1960, an occupier owes a duty of reasonable care to anyone who enters on his property, in respect of dangers due to the state of the premises, etc. for which he is responsible. This means that if the premises are in a dangerous state, either because of neglect, or because of something done by the occupier, liability will be owed to anyone entering the property who suffers harm.

The definition of occupier is the person who is in possession of the premises, or who has control over them; this is not necessarily the owner of the premises.

Product liability

As stated in Chapter 8, normally fault or negligence has to be proved for there to be liability in delict. However, statutes can be written in such a way as to remove the need to prove fault or negligence: this is strict liability. The Consumer Protection Act 1987 s.2 (1) provides strict liability for harm caused by defective products. This means that the pursuer does not have to prove fault on the part of the producer, but does still have to prove that the product was defective, and that it was this defect which caused the damages suffered. The definition of who is a 'producer' is quite wide, as is the definition of 'product'.

The damage which the act covers means death or personal injury as well as loss or damage to property. Pure economic loss is excluded. There is no liability for loss or damage to the product itself, or any product in which it was comprised. This would mean that, if a tumble drier were to go on fire and destroy the kitchen in which it is located, compensation would be due for the damaged kitchen, and the contents of the drier, unless the amount recoverable would be less than £275, but not for the appliance itself. Actions must be raised within three years of the pursuer becoming aware that the product was defective, but cannot be brought if more than ten years have elapsed since the product was supplied. A number of statutory defences are available to the producer, among which is the 'state of the art' defence: 'that the state of scientific and technical knowledge at the relevant time was not such that a producer of products of the same description as the product in question might be expected to have discovered the defect if it had existed in his products while they were under his control' (s.4(1)(e).

Defamation

Everyone is entitled to the protection of their reputation and to take action against anyone who harms that reputation by spreading lies about them, whether verbally or in writing. Scots law uses one term, 'defamation', to cover both situations, whereas English law uses the term 'slander' for the spoken lie and the term 'libel' where it is written. The victim of defamatory comments is entitled to damages for the harm to his reputation, and, where appropriate, to interdict to prevent any injurious publication or broadcast to take place. Where the source of the defamatory comments is outside the jurisdiction of the Scottish courts there may, in reality, be little that the courts can do. This is an area of law which has not been able to keep pace with advances in technology, such as the internet.

It is a valid defence to an action for defamation to assert that the statements complained of were true. It is not for the pursuer to prove that the statements are false; since the starting point of an action for defamation is that the statements ARE false, in addition to being malicious.

English law was updated by the Defamation Act 2013, taking it further away from the Scots law position. The Scottish Law Commission has recently published a Discussion Paper on this subject, with a deadline of 17th June 2016. We shall have to wait to see how this area of law is developed.

Liability for animals

This is another area where the law imposes strict liability on the keepers of some kinds of animals in some circumstances. The law is to be found in the Animals (Scotland) Act 1987. There used to be a distinction at common law between wild and domesticated animals, but this has largely been superseded by the Act. It remains possible to raise an action in common law for negligence, where harm is caused by animals.

Under the act, the keeper of an animal is strictly liable for any injury or damage caused by that animal, but this liability is limited, depending on the type of animal. If the animal is fierce and causes injury by an attack, such as a dog, or if it is a foraging animal which causes property damage by foraging, such as cattle, then in both instances the keeper becomes strictly liable. But if the animals behave in ways contrary to what the law expects of them, that is, the fierce animal damages property, or the foraging animal attacks, the act does not impose any liability on the keeper.

In the case of *Fairlie v Carruthers* 1996 S.L.T. (Sh. Ct.) 56, the pursuer alleged that she had been knocked down by a frisky dog. However, it was established that the dog had merely brushed against her, rather than attacking or harassing her, and so there was no liability under the Act. A similar case was *Welsh v Brady* [2009] C.S.I.H. 60. This time the pursuer was knocked down and injured by a black Labrador. She tried to establish that the actions of the dog could give rise to strict liability on the keeper under s.1 (1) (b) of the Act. However, for her to win her argument it would have been necessary to show that black Labradors are, by virtue of their physical attributes or habit, likely to injure severely or kill persons . . . unless controlled or restrained. The pursuer was allowed to lead evidence to this effect, but the court held that it was not sufficient to support her contention, and her case was dismissed. It appeared that the pursuer was mis-reading, and combining, two subsections of the Act in an attempt to make her case. The decision of the Sheriff Court was affirmed by the Inner House of the Court of Session.

Nuisance

This is a comparatively recent arrival in delict law, having emerged in the mid-eighteenth century. Nuisance is concerned with disruption to a person's enjoyment of their property, for example by noxious smells or loud music. In Scots law there is no distinction between public and private nuisance. Unlike its counterpart in English law, the Scots law of nuisance is relatively narrow in scope and is always determined on a balance of interests between the parties concerned with the nuisance, with liability being dependent on *culpa*, or blame. Liability arises where the pursuer is exposed to unreasonable conduct (usually on more than one occasion) to an extent that is *plus quam tolorabile* (more than is tolerable), taking both parties' interests into consideration.

The right protected by the doctrine of nuisance in Scots law is the right of the property owner to enjoy his property, without being disturbed, inconvenienced, or harmed by his neighbours. The remedy which a pursuer will be seeking is more likely to be interdict, rather than reparation. The harm which the pursuer is claiming for can be physical or mental, the latter being the nuisance complained of where the pursuer was suffering from the incessant barking of a neighbour's dogs in the case of *Shanlin v Collins* 1973 S.L.T. (Sh. Ct.) 21.

Conclusion

The focus of this chapter was on some of the particular delicts, building on the basis laid in Chapters 8 and 9 which discussed delictual liability more generally: these three chapters on delict amount to little more than an introduction to what is a fascinating area of Scots law; an area which is still developing, as can be seen from the most recent cases referred to.

Further reading

Black, G.,(editor), (2015) *Business Law in Scotland,* 3rd edition Edinburgh: W. Green. Chapter 10.

Cameron, G,. (2011) *Law Basics: Delict,* 4th edition Edinburgh: W. Green. Chapters 5, 6, 8 and 9.

McManus, F. and Russell, E., (2011) *Delict: a Comprehensive Guide to the Law* 2nd edition, Dundee: Dundee University Press. Chapters 9, 11, 12, 14 18, 19 and 20.

McManus, F., (2013) *Delict Essentials* 2nd edition Edinburgh: Edinburgh University Press. Chapters 3, 4, 5, 8, and 9.

Stewart, WJ., (2004) *Delict* 4th edition Edinburgh: W. Green. Chapters 8, 18, 19, 20, 21, 22, and 24.

Thomson, J., (2014) *Delictual Liability,* 5th edition Edinburgh: Bloomsbury Professional. Chapters 7, 8, 9, 10 12 and 15.

10

11 Law of Agency: Agents and Authorisation

Zeenat Beebeejaun

In today's fast-moving world, the creation of an agency and the role of agents have taken a prime and pivotal role in most commercial transactions, in order to get business deals made. This chapter will discuss each element involved in the making of an effective agency relationship, which will in turn be utilised for the benefit of the principal in an attempt to facilitate his day-to-day business transactions. In essence, the main parties we will be referring to throughout this chapter will be the principal, the agent and the third party, and how they are interlinked for the purpose of a commercial transaction.

The agency creation

■ What is an agency?

> "An agency is a *bilateral, onerous, consensual* contract whereby one party, the principal, authorizes another, the agent, to execute business on his behalf."

The agent acts on behalf of the principal and can alter the principal's legal position by binding him to a contract with the third party. In so doing, the principal may incur legal obligations to the third party through the agent, provided that the latter has acted within the scope of authority that has been conferred on him.

The three parties to an agency are therefore:

1 **The principal** – contractually bound to the third party for the purpose of the commercial transaction and contractually bound to the agent for the purpose of the agency agreement.

2 **The agent** – contractually bound to the principal and acts on behalf of the principal for the purpose of the commercial transaction.

3 **The third party** – contractually bound to the principal for the purpose of the commercial transaction.

The agency relationship looks like this: two contracts and three parties

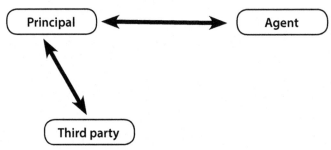

Note: Mandate is similar though not identical to agency, the main difference being that mandate is gratuitous, whereas an agent is normally paid.

Agency is widely used in business and examples include auction houses, stockbrokers, ship's captains, directors and employees of companies, solicitors, estate agents, and football and theatrical agents. Agents are much used in international business: a company in one country will often use an agent based in another to seek business for it in that country.

■ The agent

"….he who acts through another, acts himself…" in Latin, *qui facit per alium, facit per se*

This maxim implies that when an agent transacts on behalf of a principal, it is as if the principal is acting himself.

An agent shall be deemed as acting on behalf of a principal when the agent's actions bind the principal to the third party. However, an agency relationship does not arise when the agent is negotiating on his own behalf and in that event he would be eventually contractually bound to deliver to the third party in his own capacity. In that case there is no tripartite relationship.

For example, in *Spearmint Rhino Ventures (UK) Ltd v Commissioners for H.M Revenue and Customs* [2007] E.W.H.C. 613 (Ch) the defendants, Spearmint Rhino, contested a tribunal decision for the claimant (HM Revenue and Customs (HMRC)) that they had directly supplied the services of lap dancers as agents. According to HMRC, the defendants exercised control over the service fees that the dancers received from customers for dances and 'sit downs' and should therefore be liable for Value Added Tax (VAT). Mr Justice Mann held that although the dancers were paid a commission by the defendants, they were acting as 'principals' in their own right due to the fact that they separately negotiated whatever fee their services per client might render. He further declared that the dancers were not engaged as agents for the defendants since they entertained customers on their own behalf and were themselves liable to account for VAT for the services rendered.

Types of agents

There are various types of agency relationships but they are mainly categorised into general agents and special agents.

General agents:

These agents act for many functions on behalf of the principal, and have general authority to carry out all business for the principal, or all business of a particular type. They therefore have implied authority to contract on behalf of their principal, without needing express instructions, as will be discussed later in this chapter. Masters (captains) of ships are a good example: in the days before modern communications, ships often encountered problems far from their home ports, and captains had to make rapid decisions about the sale of perishable cargoes, or about getting repairs done to the ship, without being able to get express instructions from the principal. Other examples of general agents include solicitors and mercantile agents.

Special agents

These agents act on behalf of the principal for a specific function.

Mercantile agents

They operate in trade on behalf of the principal and are remunerated on the basis of a share of the profits (commission) on the sale or purchase of goods. They are divided into **factors** and **brokers.** A factor would have a

11

general lien over goods and documents of title, (see Chapter 7) which can be retained until all payments have been settled by the principal, whereas brokers used not to have this, though the class of agents who the courts recognises as having a lien has expanded over time, as can be seen in the case below. Under the Factors Acts 1889– 1890, a mercantile agent can pass title to goods to a third party even where the principal would not have consented to a sale. Examples of brokers would include insurance brokers and stockbrokers, while an auctioneer is a factor, as is a property factor and a debt factor.

The expansion of the factor's lien to stockbrokers can be seen in the case of *Glendinning v Hope & Co* 1911 S.C. (HL) 73. In this case, a stockbroker bought one hundred shares on a client's instructions and was then instructed to buy a further two hundred shares. The client then changed his mind and instructed another stockbroker to buy the two hundred shares. The original brokers claimed they were entitled to retain the original one hundred shares until they were paid for work done in the second transaction. It was held that the stockbroker was entitled to retain the uncompleted stock transfer form for the shares until paid in the second transaction.

Del credere agents

They undertake to indemnify the principal if the third party fails to perform the contract, in exchange for a fee reflecting this additional service.

Estate agents

They are normally the agent of the seller of heritable property, whose task is to bring about contracts of sale with third party buyers. They are regulated by the Estate Agents Act 1979 and the Consumer Protection from Unfair Trading Regulations SI 2008/1277.

Commercial agents

This is a different classification of agents from mercantile agents, and they are regulated by and defined in the Commercial Agents (Council Directive) Regulations 1993. These regulations enact the Commercial Agents Directive 86/653 (an EU directive). The regulations apply to all commercial agencies operating in the UK regardless of the nationality of the agent. The aim is to protect commercial agents who negotiate the sale or purchase of goods on behalf of the principal. They only apply where the work done by the commercial agent is paid. Briefly, the rules are very protective of the interests of commercial agents: they set out the duties of both parties in more detail than the corresponding common law duties; they provide detailed rules about remuneration; there are provisions giving a right to a written statement of the terms of the contract; there is a right to convert a fixed-term contract into a contract for contract for an indeterminate term on expiry of that contract; there are rules on periods of notice to be provided on termination; and there are constraints on the use of restrictive covenants in these contracts.

Formation of a valid agency agreement

An agency agreement shall only be enforceable if the parties have the necessary capacity.

As discussed in Chapter 5 earlier, a person is deemed to have the necessary capacity to enter into a contractual relationship if he is:

☐ 16 years of age and above (Age of Legal Capacity (Scotland) Act 1991);

☐ of full mental capacity;

☐ not an enemy alien;

☐ not acting under force/fear/undue influence/facility and circumvention and

☐ a legal person such as an incorporated company, a Scottish partnership or one of the forms of limited partnerships.

A legal person cannot be subject to a contract made by an agent if the contract was made before that legal person was formed. In *Tinnevelly Sugar Refining Co Ltd* v *Mirrlees, Watson & Yaryan Co Ltd* (1894) 21 R. 1009, two men bought machinery from the defenders, claiming to be acting on behalf of the pursuer company.

The company was not in fact registered until two weeks later. When the machinery was supplied, the company tried to sue as a result of a defect in the supply. It was held that the pursuer (the company) had no rights under the contract because it was not a party to it since it was not in existence and was not registered at the time of the contract.

Agency is not one of those contracts that has special formalities attached to it, and it can be created in any way in which its existence can be provide, e.g. by words and actions as well as by a written contract.

11

The agent's authority

■ ## Express authority

The most common way of forming an agency relationship between the principal and the agent is when the principal expressly consents by word and authorizes the agent to act on his behalf.

It is essential to note that the agent's scope of authority will be ascertained from the written or oral agreement between the parties and will revolve around the nature and course of business between the two parties together with the customs of the relevant trade in question.

In *Freeman & Lockyer v Buckhurst Park Properties Ltd* [1964] 2 Q.B. 480, Lord Justice Diplock explained actual authority as:

> "… a legal relationship between the principal and the agent created
> by a consensual agreement to which they alone are parties. Its scope
> is to be ascertained by applying ordinary principles of construction
> of contracts, including any proper implications from the express
> words used, the usages of the trade, or the course of business
> between the two parties …"

Therefore the principal and agent will be held as having agreed to the extent of their contractual relationship and the principal will be barred from denying that he had given express authority to the agent, at the time of the alleged creation of the agency, in order to protect the reasonable expectations of the third party.

A few examples of day-to-day actual express authority being conferred to the agent by the principal are:

1 *Employer/employee relationship*: an employer gave authority to his manager through a written document to purchase raw material up to £2.000.

2 *Auctioneer*: an antiques owner, the principal, orally appoints the auctioneer to organize an auction on his behalf.

Implied authority

An agency relationship can also be created through *implied authority* and it is normally implemented upon inference of the conduct of both parties namely the principal and the agent, and the particular circumstances. Such a situation may arise when a person, the agent, has been appointed as a managing director by the board members of a company, the principal. A managing director will be recognised as having the implied authority to carry out those transactions, which are reasonably expected to fall within the usual scope of authority of a person in that position. In other words, the agent usually carries with him the implied authority to take all decisions in favour of the company and its members without having had an express agreement conferring this authority on him. The authority was awarded by conduct. In this case, conduct was demonstrated upon his appointment as the managing director by the board members.

Other examples of agents with implied authority are partners in a partnership under s. 5 of the Partnership Act 1890, and solicitors in relation to some contracts they make as part of their agency work, such as certain searches of registers that have to be carried out when houses are being sold. A solicitor has been recognised as having implied authority to take various procedural steps in court once the principal has authorised the bringing of a legal action, but express authority may be needed to make an appeal or to settle the matter of the action, though the evidence in the individual case may demonstrate the agent has power to do these things, as shown in the case of *Riverford Finance Ltd v Kelly* 1991 S.L.T. 300 (OH), below.

In *Hely-Hutchinson v Brayhead Ltd* [1968] 1 Q.B. 549, the chairman of a company acted as its managing director although he had never been appointed to that role. He signed, on behalf of the company, contracts of guarantee and indemnity contracts. When the company refused to perform such contracts, it was held that it was bound by the contracts because it had, by conduct, granted to the chairman the implied authority of a managing director to bind the company in such a way.

Lord Denning further emphasized the actual authority present by stating that the fact that the board members had let the chairman continue to act as a managing director, had in fact created actual implied authority.

He further added that:

"…actual authority is express or implied. It is express when it is given by words, such as when a board of directors pass a resolution which authorizes two of their number to sign cheques. It is implied when it is inferred from the conduct of the parties and the circumstances of the case, such as when the board of directors appoint the managing director. They therefore impliedly authorize him to do all such things which fall within the scope of authority of that office. Actual authority, express or implied, is binding as between the company and the agent, and also as between the company and third parties…"

The board members neither opposed the entering of these contracts nor the chairman's *de facto* role as a managing director and it can be inferred from this that they had acquiesced in his acting as a managing director for the company. Such a conduct on their behalf would lead to implied authority conferred on the chairman/managing director to act in the manner that he did, thereby binding the company to the third party.

■ Further cases on implied authority

In *Barry, Ostlere & Shepherd Ltd v Edinburgh Cork Importing Co* 1909 S.C. 1113, Barry, Ostlere and Shepherd negotiated with the salesman of the Edinburgh Cork Co for the sale of some cork shavings. A contract was made but the Cork Co did not deliver. The price of shavings had then risen and Barry, Ostlere & Shepherd brought an action for breach of contract against the Cork Co. The Cork Co claimed that the salesman had not been intended to actually conclude the contract.

It was held the pursuers were entitled to assume that the salesman had the authority to complete a contract.

In *Riverford Finance Ltd* v *Kelly* 1991 S.L.T. 300 (OH), Kelly brought a Sheriff Court action against Riverford Finance Ltd in which he was granted decree by default because Riverford Finance Ltd's solicitor failed to attend the hearing. Riverford Finance Ltd's solicitor then appealed to the sheriff principal, but failed to attend the hearing of the appeal, which was then refused. He then lodged an appeal to the Court of Session, naming solicitors in Edinburgh to act in the appeal. They stated they were not prepared to act and the appeal was abandoned. Riverside Finance Ltd argued that the appeal proceedings ought to be nullified because they had given their agent no authority to bring the appeal, as by failure to pursue the appeal, the solicitors had lost Riverside its only chance of obtaining a remedy.

The court held that the solicitor needed no special authority to bring the appeal, since that was implied by the nature of his job.

■ The agent's apparent/ostensible authority (holding out)

Apparent or ostensible authority arises where the principal has given the third party to believe that the agent has authority, whereas in fact he has not. This may arise by the representation of the principal or by actings. In these cases, the agent is 'held out' as having the requisite authority to make the transaction.

An agent may still be able to bind the principal even where no authority has been conferred on him either expressly or impliedly. Such contracts between the principal and the ultimate third party will be enforceable if the agent is perceived by the third party, as having the apparent authority to enter into commercial transactions of that particular nature on behalf of the principal. Perhaps the agent formerly had wider authority and it has been reduced, or the agent's authority was restricted, but the principal allowed transactions to be made by the agent beyond the limits in previous transactions: that agent might now have apparent authority to transact beyond those limits in a future transaction with the same third party.

In *Freeman & Lockyer v Buckhurst Properties Ltd* [1964] 2 Q.B. 480, Diplock L.J. defined apparent authority as:

"a legal relationship between the principal and the [third party] created by a representation, made by the principal to the third party, intended to be and in fact acted upon by the third party, that the agent has authority to enter on behalf of the principal into a contract of a kind within the scope of 'apparent' authority, so as to render the principal liable to perform any obligations imposed upon him by such contract... The representation, when acted upon by the third party by entering into a contract with the agent, operated as an estoppel, preventing the principal from asserting that he is not bound by the contract. It is irrelevant whether the agent had actual authority to enter into the contract."

It is important to note that the doctrine of estoppel is an English doctrine and does not apply in Scotland. However, its equivalent in Scots law is known

11

as the doctrine of personal bar, which is of similar functional importance to the doctrine of estoppel with a few distinctions which will not discussed further, in line with this textbook's objectives.

The essence of the doctrine of personal bar is to protect the legitimate expectations of honest men, and students will normally come across the term *'barred'* instead of *'estopped'* whilst reading Scots cases.

In the *Freeman & Lockyer v Buckhurst Park Properties* case, Buckhurst Park Properties' articles of association provided for the appointment of a managing director with authority to bind the company by himself. No managing director was ever appointed, but one director in fact carried out this role with the approval of the other directors. He employed the plaintiffs as architects and the company refused to pay their fees, claiming that the director had no authority to employ the architects without the consent of the other directors.

It was held that the director had been **held out** by the company as having the authority to act and the company was therefore personally barred from denying that he had authority to bind the company.

Apparent authority normally arises when the principal makes a representation, which has the effect of leading the third party into believing that the agent has authority to act on his behalf. This can be contrasted with actual authority, which is derived from an agreement between the principal and the agent. Here the third party has been induced into entering the contract with the principal through an agent who appears to have the authority but in fact has no such authority.

For an agency to be created by apparent or ostensible authority (holding out), three elements must be present:

1 **There must be a representation made by the principal to the third party** to the effect that the agent has authority to act on his behalf;

2 **There must be a reliance on the representation made by the principal** which induces the third party to enter into a commercial transaction;

3 **There must be an alteration of the third party's position.**

The representation made by the principal will normally arise by conduct. In this case, conduct would constitute placing an agent in a position that would normally carry the requisite authority and one where the third party is entitled to assume that such an agent has the necessary authority, in the absence of notice to the contrary.

An example of apparent or ostensible authority could arise if an agent has been appointed to act on behalf of the principal and this is made known to the third party who has eventually entered into a commercial transaction with the latter through the agent. The agency is subsequently not renewed but the agent continues to act as if he has the authority and enters into another commercial transaction with the third party who has not been made aware of the termination. In such an event, the principal is nonetheless bound by the agent's act since the agent has still been portrayed and held out as having the authority of acting on his behalf as a result of the principal failing to notify the third party of the termination.

A representation *by the agent* of having wider authority than he has does not bring about apparent authority. In the case of *Armagas Ltd v Mundogas* [1986] A.C. 717 (HL), the House or Lords held that where an agent is known to have no general authority to enter into transactions but he falsely represented to the third party that he had obtained from the principal specific authority to enter into a one off transaction, the principal would not be bound by the agent's actions.

In *International Sponge Importers v Watt & Sons* 1911 S.C. (HL) 57, a travelling salesman for the sponge importers sold sponges. He had no authority to receive payment except by means of crossed cheques made out to the company. Watt & Sons had bought sponges from the salesman and paid by cheques made out to the salesman. The sponge company knew of this but had not objected. On one occasion Watt paid the salesman £120 in cash. It transpired that the salesman had been taking the money for himself. The sponge company tried to sue Watt & Sons for the amount that they should have received for the sponges but which the salesman had taken.

It was held that Watt & Sons were not liable to pay since they had no reason to believe that the salesman was not authorized to receive payment by this method, especially as the sponge company had not objected in the past.

In *Watteau v Fenwick* [1893] 1 QB 346, the manager of a pub was prohibited from buying goods for the business. All goods were to be supplied to the principal, his employer. The manager ordered certain articles from a supplier, which the principal refused to pay for because the manager had no authority.

11

It was held that the principal had to pay since ordering of goods was within the usual authority of a pub manager and the supplier did not know of any limitations.

In *Racing UK Ltd* v *Doncaster Racecourse Ltd* [2005] E.W.C.A. Civ. 999, Doncaster racecourse was owned by Doncaster local authority but managed by a company, Doncaster Racecourse Ltd (DRL). DRL had entered into an agreement with Racing UK, granting them television picture rights. Exercise of the rights required Racing UK to have access to the racecourse, and access could only be granted by the local authority, as owners of the course. The local authority claimed it was not bound by the agreement because DRL had no authority to make it and Racing UK had entered into the agreement with DRL in the belief that DRL was the principal.

It was held that Racing UK had known that the local authority was the owner of the racecourse and had not dealt with DRL on the basis that DRL was the principal. The evidence showed that Racing UK thought that DRL had the authority to act as agent for the local authority and that the local authority had held the chief executive of DRL out as having authority to deal with the television rights. The local authority was therefore bound by DRL's agreement with Racing UK.

In *British Bata Shoe Co Ltd* v *Double M Shah Ltd* 1980 S.C. 311, the pursuers had supplied goods to the defender, who had made payment to the pursuer's cashier who had no authority to receive payment. The cashier asked for the payee's name to be left blank on the cheque, and he later stole the cheque and cashed it for himself. The pursuer sued for payment for the goods and the defender claimed they had been paid for, and the cashier had ostensible authority to receive payment.

It was held that the cashier asking for the payee's name to be left blank on the cheque was suspicious enough that the defender should have checked whether he had authority. The defender had to pay again.

■ Actual authority v ostensible authority

Ostensible authority may sometimes exceed actual authority when for instance, the board members of a company have limited the agent's authority, by asking him to seek their approval for any transactions of £1,000 and above but his ostensible authority includes all the usual authority of a managing director. Therefore, even though his actual authority is bound by the

£1,000 limitation, the company is bound by his ostensible authority for those who have not been made aware of the limitation. The case of *International Sponge Importers v Watt & Sons* is an example of this.

Exercise

Sid has a long-standing contract with Jane under which Jane purchases quality used cars for Sid. The agreement is for her to be able to make purchases of up to £10,000, but purchases above that level need to be authorised by Sid. In fact, recently Jane has bought several cars for prices just above that limit, but Sid did not object. Jane is a well-known figure around the car sales and auction rooms, though none of the dealers knows of the financial restriction on Jane's dealings.

Last week Jane bought a second hand Range Rover for £15,000. Sid has refused to pay for this, on the ground that the price was above what he had agreed.

Will Sid be liable to pay for this car or can he reject it in the ground that Jane had no authority as agent to make the contract?

Agency of necessity

■ How does it arise?

An agency of necessity might occur when one party (the agent) has acted on behalf of another (the principal) during an emergency.

The following requirements are needed before an agency of necessity is established:

☐ Genuine necessity

☐ Communication is impossible

☐ Actions must be in the interests of the principal

The emergency must have represented such an imminent threat to the principal's property that the agent genuinely needed to have acted immediately without there being any means of communication or time left for him to seek consent from the principal.

The authority that arises in an agency of necessity is *presumed authority*: it is presumed from the facts of the case. Nowadays, with good communications, it will rarely be the case that communication is impossible, and therefore these cases are unlikely to arise.

11

The case of *Great Northern Railway* v *Swaffield* (1873-74) L.R. 9 Exch. 132 is a clear example of an agent genuinely acting for the benefit of the principal in a situation where communication with the latter has become impossible.

A railway company was hired to deliver a horse on behalf of S, the principal. The horse arrived late and night and was put into livery stables until the owner could collect it. The owner arrived shortly after and refused to pay the charges, insisting that the horse be delivered to his farm at the railway company's expense. As a result, the horse remaining in the stables for several months. The railway company paid the cost of the horse's stay in the livery stables, and sued S for recovery of the money. It was held that S was liable pay the livery costs since putting the horse in stables was a reasonable act done out of necessity, considering the welfare of the horse.

■ Contrast

In the case of *Springer* v *Great Western Railway Co* [1921] 1 K.B. 257, the agent, Great Western Railway, had been contracted to carry a consignment of tomatoes from Jersey to London. The ship was late in arriving and when it did, the agent's employees were on strike. When the cargo was unloaded, some of the tomatoes had gone bad and the agent decided to sell the whole consignment locally.

It was held that the agent was not acting out of necessity in selling the tomatoes since communication was not impossible at the time that the decision needed to be taken. Such an action by the agent was not *bona fide* and can also not be construed as acting in the best interests of the principal.

The agent was then liable to pay the owners for the losses incurred.

A Scottish case on presumed authority is *Fernie v Robertson* (1891) 9 M. 437. In this case a frail elderly lady was looked after by her daughter in her own home. The daughter organised repairs on her behalf as agent, and had been granted a deed by her mother under which she was to inherit the property. However, on the mother's death, her son repudiated the deed and insisted on inheriting himself, and refused to pay for the repairs. The court held that the son was liable to meet these payments ordered by his sister, as agent for her mother, as he could have stopped the work at the time, as he also lived in the house, and if he wanted to inherit the house he needed to pay the repairs.

Agency by ratification

■   The concept of ratification

A principal might decide to acknowledge an agent's previous unauthorised act as a result of which an agency relationship will be created retrospectively. In such an event, the principal is said to have ratified the agent's past actions, therefore authorising and adopting the agent's acts and subsequently being bound to the third party.

In *Koenigsblatt* v *Sweet* [1923] 2.Ch. 314, Lord Sterndale M.R. explained ratification in the following terms:

> "once you get a ratification, it relates back; it is equivalent to an antecedent authority:... and when there has been ratification the act that is done is put in the same position as if it had antecedently been authorised."

The concept of ratification is further illustrated in the case of *Lass Salt Garvin* v *Pomeroy* [2003] E.W.H.C. 1007, where the claimants were a firm of solicitors seeking to recover fees of £100,000 for acting in connection with the sale of shares from one company to another. Previously the claimant had issued invoices but the fees were not paid as they fell due. The defendants however claimed that their agent had not had authority to agree to the legal fees but the claimants claimed that the agent had been authorized to agree to the fees which he did. It was also argued that even if the agent did not have the authority to agree to the fees, the defendants' subsequent silence and failure to challenge the claimants' invoices amounted to a ratification of the agent's acts.

It was held that, on the evidence, the defendants were liable to pay the claimants' fees since although they had not authorized the agent to agree on the fees, their subsequent silence and failure to challenge the invoices until such a late stage indicated that they were prepared to ratify the agent's actions.

11

■   Requirements for ratification:

The elements required for ratification are:

Principal in existence

This requirement relates to agents who are acting on behalf of companies and it demonstrates that if an agent has acted for a company before it has been incorporated, the company once incorporated cannot then ratify the agent's acts.

The case of *Kelner v Baxter* 1866 L.R. 2 C.P. 174 depicts this further whereby three purported directors bought goods on behalf of a company yet to be formed. The company was later registered but became insolvent before the goods were paid for. It was held that the purported directors had acted without a principal, as no company was in existence at the time of the contract, and they were personally liable on the contract, the company being unable to ratify the contract.

Principal with capacity

The principal must be competent to perform the act at the time the agent acted on his behalf.

In *Boston Deep Sea Fishing and Ice Co Ltd* v *Farnham* (1957) 1 W.L.R. 1051, a trawler owned by a French company was at an English port when France became occupied by enemy forces during the Second World War. The English company carried on trade by using the trawler during the war period, purporting to act as agents of the French company, although without authority from them. At the end of the war the French company purported to ratify the English company's activities.

It was held that the principal must himself have been competent to perform the act at the time the agent acted on his behalf. The French company could not effectively ratify the English company's activities during the hostilities as the French company was at that time an alien enemy.

Ratification must be timeous

Following on from the previous requirement, the principal should also still have the right to ratify the agent's actions.

In *Goodall v Bilsland* 1909 S.C. 1152, a wine merchant applied to the licensing court to have his wine and spirits licence renewed. Opponents to the renewal employed a solicitor to act for them opposing the application.

The renewal was granted. The law allowed 10 days for an appeal against this and the solicitor, without consulting his principals, lodged an appeal, which was successful. The wine merchant appealed against this and was successful. The solicitor had no authority to bring the appeal and his doing so could not be ratified after the ten days allowed for lodging the appeal had lapsed. The appeal proceedings were therefore held to be null and void.

Agent acting as agent

Failure by the agent to disclose that he is acting on behalf of a principal would result in the principal not being bound to perform since he has not been identified at the start of the transaction and hence cannot ratify the agent's actions.

In *Keighley Maxted & Co* v *Durant* [1901] A.C. 240, K M & Co authorized a man called Roberts to buy wheat for them and himself with a limit as to the price he could pay. He failed to buy at this price and entered into a contract with the defendant, Durant, to buy at a higher price. He did not disclose to the defendant that he was acting for someone else as well as himself. K M & Co then agreed with Roberts to take the wheat at the higher price. Both K M & Co and Roberts eventually failed to take delivery and Durant sued for damages.

It was held that K M & Co could not be made liable as Durant had not known at the time the contract was made that Roberts was acting for anyone other than himself.

Principal aware of material facts

The principal must have been made aware of the material facts before ratifying the agent's actions which consequently creates a retrospective agency relationship.

Failure by the agent to make the principal aware of the material facts of the transaction would prevent the latter from relying on the acts to enforce a contract. In *Foreman & Co v the Liddesdale* [1900] A.C. 190, a Privy Council case (appeal from a court in Australia), the agent was authorised to arrange for basic repairs to be done to a damaged ship following a stranding. However, the repairs were more major than those authorised. After the repairs had been carried out, the shipowner took the ship as repaired and sold it. The court held that because the principal was not aware of all the relevant facts, its conduct in taking and selling the ship did not amount to ratification.

11

Conclusion

Agents have a very important part to play in business. They enable people to transact much more business than they could without using agents, and they also bring expertise that the principal might not have. The agency relationship involves three parties and two contracts: between principal and agent and principal and third party. The chapter discussed how contracts of agency are made, and the different kinds of authority that an agent might have.

Further reading

Ashton, C., et al., (2012) *Understanding Scots Law* 2nd edition. Edinburgh: W. Green. Chapter 10 pp.396-400.

Black, G., (ed), (2015) *Business Law in Scotland* 3rd edition. Edinburgh: W. Green. Chapter 9 pp.337-349.

Combe, M., (2013) *Law Essentials: Commercial Law* Dundee: Dundee University Press. Chapter 3 pp.31-37.

Davidson, F., and Macgregor, L., (2014) *Commercial Law in Scotland* 3rd edition. Edinburgh: W. Green. Chapter 2, pp.53-67.

Macgregor, L., (2013) *The Law of Agency in Scotland.* Edinburgh: W. Green.

12 Law of Agency: Legal Relationships

Zeenat Beebeejaun

As in most agreements, the parties are contractually bound to a set of rights and duties by which they have to abide throughout the term of the agreement. A breach of the duties by one party or failure to render any obligations by the other party could potentially lead to the termination of a contract. Rarely, the agent might find himself tied into a contract with the third party personally, though this would never be his intention. This chapter will discuss the main rights and duties of the parties involved in an agency agreement, together with the events that could result in the termination of a contract and which would lead to the dissolution of the agency arrangement.

At common law, the principal and the agent owe each other certain duties. These duties are reflected in reciprocal rights held by the other, e.g. the principal has a duty to compensate the agent and the agent has a right to compensation.

Principal's duties

■ Duty of compensation

As has been noted in Chapter 11, agency is an onerous contract. The principal has a duty to compensate the agent for the services the latter rendered. This would normally arise if the agent has acted in good faith and within the realms of the authority that has been conferred upon him as per the agency agreement. Compensation might be in the form of a commission on sales, or a fee, depending on the terms of the contract or customs of the trade.

The following cases are authority for the duty of compensation of the principal:

In *Kennedy* v *Glass* (1890) 17 R. 1085, Glass was a dealer in old machinery and Kennedy was an architect who had often introduced Glass to people who had old machinery for sale and had been paid for this. On one occasion, Kennedy introduced Glass to a company which had machinery and plant for sale. Glass entered into a contract with the company to buy it but failed to carry out the contract. Kennedy said there had been an arrangement that he would get £250 commission. Glass said it was £50, and only if the contract was carried out.

The court held that Kennedy was entitled to £50 on a *quantum meruit* basis ("as much as it is worth") as he had taken considerable time and trouble on Glass's behalf.

In *Way* v *Latilla* [1937] 3 All E.R. 759 (H.L), Way agreed to send to Latilla information about gold mines in Africa and, in return, Way would receive a concession in any gold mine that Latilla obtained. However, the agency agreement was silent in relation to the remuneration that Way would receive and Latilla denied offering Way a concession.

The court held that Latilla should be compensated on a *quantum merit* basis since the work done by the agent was not to be gratuitous.

In *PJ Pipe & Valve Co Ltd* v *Audco India Ltd* [2005] E.W.H.C. 1904 (QB), the claimants had two agency agreements with the defendant, one of which did not make any provision for the rate of commission to be paid. When this agreement was terminated by the defendant, the claimants brought a claim for compensation for commission outstanding in respect of orders placed for a project. Expert evidence showed that the usual commission level in industry was 5%, but lower levels were paid for high value orders, which this was.

The court held the claimants were entitled to a commission of 4.5%.

■ Duty of reimbursement

The principal owes a duty of reimbursement to the agent in the event that the agent has incurred out-of-pocket expenses, in the reasonable performance of his agent's duties. It is important to note that such a duty can be challenged if the agent has not acted in good faith and/or has exceeded the authority that has been conferred upon him.

In *Drummond* v *Cairns* (1852) 14 D. 611, Cairns was a stockbroker who was instructed by Drummond to buy certain shares. He bought them and told Drummond he had done so, but when the time came to pay the price, Drummond refused to pay. Cairns then sold the shares, but the price had fallen. The court held that Drummond was liable to repay Cairns the difference in the two prices.

In *Tomlinson* v *Scottish Amalgamated Silks Ltd* 1935 S.C. (H.L.) 1, Tomlinson was a director of Scottish Amalgamated Silks Ltd. The articles of association of Scottish Amalgamated Silks Ltd allowed for a director to be indemnified by the company against all losses and expenses incurred in performance of his duties as director. The company then went into liquidation and Tomlinson was tried for fraudulently using the funds of the company. He was acquitted, and lodged a claim in the liquidation for the costs of defending the case. The court held he was not entitled to reclaim this since the expenses were not incurred in the performance of his duties as a director.

■ Duty to relieve agent from legitimately incurred liability

The principal owes a duty of relief to the agent in circumstances whereby the agent has acted in good faith and in the best interest of the principal without exceeding the authority that has been conferred upon him.

It is perhaps stating the obvious to say that an agent would be deemed as being personally liable for any expenses he may have incurred as a result of him acting beyond the scope of authority given to him by the principal.

In *Rhodes* v *Fielder, Jones & Harrison* [1919] ALL E.R. 846, a firm of country solicitors employed a firm of London solicitors to brief counsel. After the case, the country solicitors instructed the London solicitors to withhold payment of counsel's fees. Nevertheless, the London solicitors paid the fees and claimed to be entitled to an indemnity.

The court held in this case that the London solicitors were employed as solicitors and to fail to pay counsel would be deemed as professional misconduct. Therefore, they were entitled to go against the principal's instructions in order to act properly. In the circumstances, they were entitled to be indemnified (reimbursed).

In *Marshall, Wilson Dean & Turnbull* v *Feymac Properties Ltd* 1996 G.W.D. 22 1247, the pursuers were solicitors instructed by the defenders to act in the sale of property belonging to the defenders. Before the sale could be completed, certain planning documents had to be produced, and the defenders told the solicitors that these were about to be issued. The solicitors granted a letter of obligation to the purchasers on the strength of this assertion however, such documents were never forthcoming and the solicitors had to pay for work to be carried out before they would be granted.

The court held the defenders were liable to compensate the pursuers for the expense of having the work done and for their costs in defending the action brought against them by the purchasers of the property.

Contrast

In *Robinson* v *Middleton* (1859) 21 D. 1089, Middleton instructed Robinson to sell some wood for him. Robinson sold the wood to Perry, the latter being the agent of an Australian firm. Perry and Robinson made an arrangement that Perry would not incur any liability on the transaction, but this arrangement was not told to Middleton. The price for the wood was paid by bill of exchange drawn by Perry on the Australian firm, but this firm became insolvent by the time the wood was delivered. The bank which had discounted the bill sold the wood, but only got a price £1000 less than the amount of the bill. Normally Perry, as drawer of the bill, would have been liable to make up the amount, but he had been released from liability by Robinson so the latter paid the £1000 and tried to claim it from Middleton.

The court held Middleton did not have to pay as he had not consented to Perry being released from any liability on the bill.

■   Duty of good faith and fair dealing

Upon entering into a contract of agency, the principal has a duty to cooperate with the agent and deal with the agent fairly and honestly for the proper performance of the agent's duties.

Where the agency is governed by the Commercial Agents (Council Directive) Regulations 1993, the principal must act dutifully and in good faith towards the commercial agent, in terms of regulation 4.

Agent's duties

■ Duty to obey instructions

Generally, an agent is under a duty to obey the lawful instructions of the principal and should render his services without exceeding his authority. Unless the agent is an expert in the field of practice in which the services are being expected to be rendered and the principal relies on the agent's knowledge to complete the task, the agent does not have any discretion but to follow the instructions given by the principal.

Failure to obey instructions will inevitably result in the agent being personally liable for the loss incurred by the principal and forfeit his right of remuneration.

In *Gilmour* v *Clark* (1853) 15 D. 478, Gilmour gave instructions to Clark, a carrier, to take goods to the docks and put them on a ship called the *Earl of Zetland*. Clark put them on a ship called *The Magnet* instead and this ship sank and the goods were lost. Clark was held to be liable to Gilmour for the value of the goods.

In *Graham & Co* v *United Turkey Red Co* 1922 S.C. 533, it was a term of the contract that the agent was not to sell goods supplied by anyone other than the principal. The agent sold other goods and was dismissed. It was held in that case that the agent was not entitled to commission for the period when he sold other supplier's goods.

■ Duty not to delegate

Owing to the fact that an agency agreement is between the principal and the agent, and that authority is normally given to the agent personally, on account of his trustworthiness, skill or experience (*delectus personae*), the agent is under a duty to the principal not to delegate his duties unless the latter expressly or impliedly authorises the agent to appoint a sub-agent.

In *De Bussche* v *Alt* [1878] 8 Ch. 286, the principal, De Bussche, appointed an agent to sell a ship in China at a certain price. The agent also had authority to appoint a sub-agent and he appointed Alt to try to sell the ship in Japan. It was held this was not a breach of the agent's duty, and, as Alt had been appointed as a substitute for the original agents, there was a contract between De Bussche and Alt. This case is also referred to the next section of this chapter in relation to the agent's fiduciary duties.

12

■   Fiduciary duties: loyalty and good faith

Agents owe positive duties of loyalty and good faith to the principal. These are fiduciary duties. The agent owes a duty to act in the principal's best interests and the courts in general tend not to depart from this rule.

In relation to commercial agents, regulation 3 of the Commercial Agents (EC Directive) Regulations 1993 states:

> " In performing his activities a commercial agent must look after the interests of his principal and act dutifully and in good faith."

In *Rossetti and Anor v Diamond Sofa Company Ltd* [2013] 1 All E.R. (Comm.) 308, Diamond was a company manufacturing leather upholstery and it entered into an agency agreement with SML which was set up to represent furniture manufacturers. Both parties had orally agreed that SML would act as their exclusive agent and SML informed Diamond, during the course of negotiation, that it was already acting for two other manufacturers of upholstery, which were however specialized in other categories of furniture, neither of them being direct competitors to Diamond. During the course of the agency agreement, SML's business was transferred to RML and Diamond continued to rely on the agency for the purpose of representing their upholstery until it came to light that RML was working for other principals which were in direct competition to Diamond. The latter brought an action for breach of loyalty and good faith. The case was regulated by the Commercial Agents (EC Directive) Regulations 1993.

It was held in the Court of Appeal that since Diamond had not agreed to SML working for its direct competitors and had requested SML to be their exclusive agent, this resulted in a fundamental breach of SML's duty of loyalty and good faith.

Contrast

In *Lothian v Jenolite Ltd* 1969 S.C. 111, Lothian agreed with Jenolite Ltd to sell some of Jenolite's products in Scotland in exchange for commission. The agreement was for a four year period but Jenolite ended it after a little over a year. Lothian brought a claim for damages for breach of contract and Jenolite counterclaimed by saying that Lothian had bought and sold competitors' products, and that he was therefore himself in breach of contract.

The court held the contract had not stated that Lothian should only sell Jenolite's products and he was entitled to also sell those of a competitor.

Notably, Jenolite had not appointed Lothian as their exclusive agent whereas Diamond did appoint SML as their exclusive agent.

As will be seen, this fiduciary duty is very strict. Such duty encompasses three aspects namely:

☐ An agent must not transact with the principal on his own behalf

☐ An agent must not receive any profit, commission or benefit from the third party

☐ Agent owes a duty of confidence in respect of information gained through the agency

An agent must not transact with the principal on his own behalf

In *McPherson's Trustees* v Watt [1877] 5 R. (H.L.) 9, Watt was a solicitor who bought four houses from the trustees for his brother. Watt was also the solicitor for the trustees and before the sale was made, Watt had arranged with his brother that he would pay him half the price and take two of the houses for himself.

The court held that Watt had made the contract without disclosing to the trustees that he was partly buying for himself and the transaction was therefore set aside by the court.

The court also pointed out that it did not matter if the bargain was a good one or not as the sale would still be set aside if Watt had paid a fair price.

In *Lucifero* v *Castel* [1887] T.L.R. 371, the agent was asked to purchase a yacht for his principal but he first bought a yacht for himself and then resold it to his principal at a profit. The principal was unaware that he was buying the agent's own property until later.

It was held that the agent must give up the profit he had made and he was only allowed to retain the price he had paid for the yacht.

An agent must not receive any profit, commission or benefit from the third party otherwise the following consequences may follow:

1 The principal can claim the benefit.

In *Ronaldson* v *Drummond & Reid* (1881) 8 R. 956, a solicitor, acting for a client, employed an auctioneer to sell furniture. The auctioneer paid the solicitor a percentage of the commission he took for the sale, but the solicitor did not pass the benefit of that discount on to his client. The court held that he was obliged to do so.

In *De Bussche* v *Alt* [1878] 8 Ch. D. 286, Alt was employed as a sub-agent to sell a ship in Japan for a minimum price of $90,000. He told the original agents that he did not think that he could sell it but offered to buy it himself for the sum of $90,000. The ship was sold to him at that price, but he had in fact negotiated a sale to a Japanese prince for $160,000.

It was held that Alt was in breach of his fiduciary duty and he was obliged to account to the principal for the profit he had made.

In *FHR European Ventures LLP & Others* v *Cedar Capital Partners (LLC)* [2015] A.C. 250, the claimant was the purchaser of the issued share capital of Monte Carlo Grand Hotel and the agent was representing the latter in the purchase. However, the agent had made a deal with Monte Carlo Grand Hotel Ltd (the seller) that he would receive a commission of 10 million euros following the successful purchase. The claimant sought to recover the 10 million euros once he became aware of the deal.

It was held that a bribe or secret commission accepted by an agent is held on trust for his principal; not only did the principal have a right to sue the sum equal to the benefit the agent had received but that the principal had a proprietory interest in that benefit as well as a personal remedy against the defendant.

2   Thw agent loses his commission and may be dismissed

In *Hippisley* v *Knee Bros* [1905] 1 KB 1, the defendant auctioneers were employed by the plaintiff to sell some goods. The payment was to be a percentage commission with a minimum of £20 and 'all out of pocket' expenses for advertising. The sale triggered the £20 commission and the auctioneers' bill included that plus the gross cost of the advertisements. The auctioneers had in fact received a discount on the cost of advertising but did not disclose this in the bill, in the mistaken and honest belief that there was a custom which entitled them to this, the point being that if the client had ordered the advertisements directly, no discount would have been given. The bill was paid in full and the plaintiff later discovered that there had been a discount and he sued not only for the amount but for the £20 commission.

It was held the agent would lose his commission if he had acted in bad faith and if such an action on his part was related to the duty in question. In the current case, the commission was earned as a result of the sale of some goods and the agents acted faithfully in the performance of that duty, which entitled them to earn the commission. The advertising duty was seen as another duty to be performed by the agents and here, the courts held in favour of the plaintiff and awarded the sum of the discount to him.

Lord Alverstone further stated that if the commission was connected to the contract in question, such commission would be forfeited if the agent had acted fraudulent and dishonestly.

In *Kelly* v *Cooper* [1993] A.C. 205, Lord Browne-Wilkinson observed that an agent will lose his right to commission where the breach of his fiduciary duties was dishonesty, or if honest, the breach went to root of the agent's obligations.

A recent case concerning the consequences for the agent of seeking a secret commission is *Daraydan Holdings Ltd v Solland Ltd* [2005] Ch. 119. In this case, K was an agent of M, a Qatari national who held property in England, and was tasked with arranging the refurbishment of M's properties. He negotiated with the defendants, who agreed to pay 10% commission, on the basis that the contract price would be inflated to cover the commission, to conceal it from M. The commission amounted to £1.8m, and the defendants fraudulently misrepresented that the sum payable covered the cost of the refurbishment only. One of the defendants was a company which had been set up simply to be a vehicle to channel the secret commission to K.

The court held that K was in breach of his fiduciary duties and a restitutionary remedy was appropriate here. It was also at pains to stress that there were powerful reasons of public policy why it was important to ensure that a fiduciary is not able to retain property gained in breach of fiduciary duty.

3 Principal may be able to claim damages from the third party and rescind the contract

Where profit, commission or benefit has been received by the agent from the third party, the principal has the right to rescind the contract and claim for damages. This was confirmed by *Taylor* v *Walker* [1958] 1 Lloyd's Rep. 490 and later followed by *Logicrose Ltd* v *Southend United Football Club (No2)* [1988] 1 W.L.R. 1256.

4   There are criminal penalties for bribery under The Bribery Act 2010 for both the third party and the agent.

12

The agent owes a duty of confidence in respect of information gained through the agency

It is a breach of fiduciary duty if the agent uses information acquired during the agency for his own personal advantage or for the benefit of a third party.

In *Liverpool Victoria Friendly Society* v *Houston* (1900) 3F. 42, Houston was an agent of Liverpool Victoria for 4 years, during which time he saw lists of people insured by them. He was dismissed and then offered the lists to a rival society, which canvassed the people on them.

It was held that Houston had a duty to treat the information in the lists as confidential and could not use them against his principal. He was liable in damages for loss of business suffered by Liverpool Victoria as a result.

■ Duty of care and skill

It is required at common law for an agent to act with reasonable care and skill whilst performing his duties. The standard of care will vary, depending whether or not the agent is a professional. Where the principal is a consumer, under s. 49 of the Consumer Rights Act 2015, the contract will be treated as including a term that the agent must display reasonable care and skill in carrying out services. The following case is an example of breach of the duty of care and skill at common law.

In *Salvesen & Co v Rederi Aktibolaget Nordstjiernan* (1905) 7 F. (H.L.) 101, a shipowner had contracted with a shipbroker to find a cargo for his vessel. The shipowner was expecting to be able to go on and resell the cargo for a profit. The shipbroker falsely stated that a contract had been completed whereas in fact this was not the case. The shipowner therefore sued for damages, for the loss of profit that would have been made on the sale of the cargo to the coal merchant. The House of Lords held where the agent makes an incorrect statement to the principal that it has concluded a bargain on its behalf, damages could be claimed for the loss sustained by the principal, but not loss of the profit that might have been made had the contract for the cargo been concluded.

■ Duty to account

An agent has a duty to account to the principal of any property received by him in the course of the agency. Such a duty may continue after the term of the agency.

In *Tyler* v *Logan* (1904) 7F. 123, Logan was the manager of a branch of a shoe shop. During stocktaking, there was a shortfall of £62.

It was held Logan was obliged to pay this amount to Tyler even though there was no evidence of dishonesty or negligence since he failed to provide an explanation which would account for the loss.

In *John Youngs Insurance Services Ltd* v *Aviva Insurance Services UK Ltd* [2012] 1 All E.R. (Comm.) 1045, John Youngs had entered into an agreement with Aviva to provide claims-handling services to Aviva and building repair services for policy holders. Following termination of the agreement, John Youngs brought proceedings against Aviva for unpaid invoices and other costs, upon which Aviva issued a counterclaim, arguing that John Youngs had provided insufficient records and documents to prove their claim and that they owed Aviva a fiduciary duty of enquiry and account which survived termination of the agreement.

It was held the fiduciary duty survived the termination of the agency agreement and John Youngs was accountable to Aviva on the provision of the documents requested by Aviva.

■ Duty of relief

This duty arises as a result of the agent's failure to obey the principal's instructions, as a result of which the principal incurs liability.

In *Milne* v *Ritchie* (1882) 10 R. 365, Milne was an architect who had authority to negotiate and contact for mason work up to a value of £1465. Milne accepted Ritchie's offer to do the work for £1646 and Ritchie brought a successful action to make Milne's principal pay the £1646. The court held the principal was entitled to be relieved of his loss by Milne.

Exercise

Fred has worked for many years as the agent of Mary, organizing repairs to Mary's commercial properties. He does this work for various other principals as well. In the course of his work, various other companies grant Fred discount for repeat business. However, Fred has always invoices Mary and the other principals for the full amount, on the basis that they would not qualify for the discount if they arranged these contracts themselves. Mary has now found out what has been going on.

Advise Fred on his legal position, applying the rules on the duties of an agent.

12

Rights and liabilities of third parties

Normally, when an agent is involved in the making of a contract on behalf of a principal, the resulting contract is between the principal and the third party. Normally the agent does not face any personal liability on that contract. However, there are circumstances in which the resulting contract ends up being between the third party and the agent may be liable to the third party for breach of warranty of authority, in other words, wrongly stating that he had authority as agent to make the contract for the principal.

■   Agent transacting as agent for named principal

This is the normal case – the third party is told that the agent is acting for a named principal. The general rule is that only the principal and the third party have right and liabilities under the contract effected by the agent. This rule applies as long as the agent had express or implied authority to bind the principal and the principal's existence was disclosed to the third party. Where this is the case, the agent will not incur liability on the transaction.

In *Stone & Rolfe* v *Kimber Coal Co* 1926 S.C. (H.L.) 45, the coal company acted as agents to charter a ship for a Scandinavian company. The contract was signed by a representative of the Coal Co, the signature was preceded by the words "For the Atlantic Baltic Co" (the Scandinavian company). The third party brought an action against the coal company for certain expenses incurred.The court held that the coal company were not liable as they had clearly signed as agents only.

In *Armour* v TL *Duff & Co* 1912 S.C. 120, the owners of a ship and its brokers ordered goods to be supplied to that particular ship. The suppliers then sent the invoice to the brokers (the agents), believing they were the owners of the ship and the brokers refused to pay.

The court held the agents were not liable. They had effectively been acting as agents for a disclosed principal since the suppliers could have ascertained the name of the ship owners from the Register of Shipping.

■   Agent transacting for a disclosed but unnamed principal

In such cases, the agent contracts, stating that it is done as an agent, but not naming the principal. Problems arise where the third party seeks a remedy for breach of contract and does not know who the principal is. There is little authority in Scots law. However, if the identity of the principal is revealed, there is authority to the effect that the third party may choose whether to exercise remedies against the agent personally or against the principal. However, the other approach found in the Scottish case law is to focus on whether the third party is relying on the credit of the agent or the principal is making the contract. The following cases show the two approaches:

- ☐ **Approach 1: third party can choose which party to sue**. In Ferrier v Dods ([1865) 3M. 561, Dods was auctioneer and he advertised a sale of horses, warranted as good workers. Ferrier bought a horse but later informed Dods that it was unfit for work. Dods told Ferrier that he had the right to return the horse, and suggested he returns her to her former owner. Ferrier did this but did not get his money back and he then tried to sue Dods.

  By returning the horse to the owner, it was held that Ferrier had effectively elected to take action against him and the action against Dods was dismissed.

- ☐ **Approach 2: the third party has remedies against the party whose credit he relied on when contracting**. In *Lamont Nisbett & Co v Hamilton* 1907 S.C. 628, the agents owned a ship and managed various others, and arranged insurance over the ships with insurance brokers. The agents went into liquidation and the insurance brokers sought payment of the premium paid in relation to one of the ships from the owner of the ship. However, the court held on the evidence that the insurance brokers had entered into these contracts relying on the credit of the agents, and therefore they had no claim against the ship owners. If they had wanted to find out the names of the owners, they had the means of doing so by referring to the Registry of Shipping.

In *Humble v Hunter* [1848] 12 Q.B. 310, the principal authorized the agent to make a contract of charter in relation to a ship owned by the principal. The agent did make such a contract with the third party without disclosing that he was acting for a principal and describing himself in the charterparty as 'owner' of the ship.

12

It was held that the principal could not enforce the contract and to allow evidence that principal was really the owner would be to contradict the terms of the contract, and the agent had impliedly contracted that he was the only principal.

If the agent refuses to reveal the identity of the principal, the third party has the right to sue the agent.

In *Gibb* v *Cunningham & Robertson* 1925 S.L.T. 608, solicitors were contracted by a client to purchase company shares and a house belonging to the third party. The papers showed that they were acting for a client but never disclosed the identity of the client. Upon signing the contract, the purchase price was later not paid and the seller sought for the name of the client but the solicitors failed to reply.

The seller was entitled to sue the solicitors for the price since they had refused to reveal the identity of the client and had denied the seller a remedy and were therefore held to be personally liable.

■ Agent contracting for an undisclosed principal

Sometimes agents make contracts with third parties without mentioning that they are contracting as agents. Clearly, the third party would be entitled to sue the agent if he was unaware at the time of making the contract that he was contracting with an agent. However, the principal may disclose himself and exert rights under that contract. In *Bennett* v *Inveresk Paper Company* (1891) 18 R. 975, Bennett owned a newspaper in Australia and he asked his London agents to contract for the supply of paper. The latter entered into a contract with Inveresk to supply the paper and ship it to Australia. Inveresk were not aware of the existence of the principal at this time. The paper was damaged upon arrival and Bennett brought an action for breach of contract against Inveresk and it was held that he had title to sue.

The third party would also be entitled to sue the principal or the agent in such an event.

Agent contracts as agent but exceeds his actual and ostensible authority

In general, most agents who have disclosed that they are dealing on behalf of an identified principal warrant to the third party that they have been duly authorised to act and deal on their behalf.

Such a warranty is usually implied but sometimes the third party would seek an express warranty stipulating that the agent has been properly authorised by the principal to act on his behalf and enter into the proposed transaction. For example, when the directors of a new company want to open a bank account, the bank will routinely ask to see an extract of the item in the board minutes authorising this to be done.

In the event that the third party had relied on the implied warranty that the agent had the authority, and it came to light that such an authority had never been granted, the third party may bring a claim for breach of warranty of authority against the agent for any damages that the third party may have suffered as a result the agent's lack of authority.

In *Irving v Burns* 1915 S.C. 260, Burns was the secretary of a company and he claimed to have the authority of the company and accepted an offer made by Irving for plumbing work to be done at a theatre. Irving did the work and then discovered that Burns had no authority. He sued Burns for breach of warranty of authority and it transpired that the company had no assets and would not have been able to pay Irving even if he had a contract with them. As Irving would have been no better off if he had successfully made a contract with the principal, no damages were payable.

A recent case in which breach of warranty of authority was discussed is *Halifax Life Ltd v DLA Piper Scotland Ltd* [2009] C.S.O.H.74. In this case, solicitors put in an offer and concluded a bargain to purchase a commercial property in Glasgow on behalf of a syndicate which did not exist. The sellers sued the solicitors for implement of the contract or damages for breach of contract or damages for losses resulting from negligent misrepresentation. The court held that the solicitors could not be personally liable for specific implement of the contract, but the case suggested that breach of warranty of authority might be an appropriate remedy, though there was no definitive decision by the court in this case.

Termination of agency

Agency comes to an end in similar ways to any other contract, and therefore what we discussed in Chapter 7 is relevant.

■ Termination of agency by act of the parties

☐ **Mutual agreement** – the parties may at any time mutually agree to bring the agency to an end.

☐ **Revocation by the principal** – the authority of an agent may be revoked at any time by the principal. However such an act may render the principal in breach of the agency agreement if not made in accordance to the provisions of the agreement.

Revocation of an agent's authority may not automatically discharge the principal from liability to a third party who has relied on the agent's apparent authority before entering into an agreement.

☐ **Renunciation** – an agent is entitled to renounce his authority by notifying the principal in accordance to the agency agreement provisions.

Renunciation may render the agent liable to the principal for breach of contract which will result in the principal being entitled to damages.

■ Termination by operation of law

☐ **Expiry of time** – where the agency is for a period of time, termination of the agency can take place after the expiry of the agreed period.

☐ **Completion of transaction** – termination may happen upon the fulfilment of the transaction by the agent.

☐ **Material breach** – a breach of the agent's duties and obligations or a breach of the principal's duties and obligations would result in the termination of the agency.

☐ **Frustration**

- Death of principal or agent
- Insanity of principal or agent
- Bankruptcy of either party
- Enemy alien – At times of war between countries, the principal or the agent may become an enemy alien which would make it illegal to trade with the enemy.
- Cessation of principal's business

In *Patmore & Co v Cannon & Co* (1892) 19 R. 1004, Patmore agreed to act as Cannon's agents for sale of certain goods. The agency was to be for a period of five years unless broken by mutual consent and with a contract break clause at the end of the first year. After only a few months, Cannon gave up manufacturing the goods.

Patmore had no claim for breach of contract as Cannon had not undertaken to carry on the business for 5 years. The court held there was an implied condition that a contract would be brought to an end by the discontinuance of the principal's business.

Conclusion

The last two chapters explored the three-cornered relationship of principal, agent and third party. The principal and agent are in a positive fiduciary relationship, where they owe duties of loyalty and good faith to each other. This chapter also focused on what happens when things go wrong in the relationships between the three parties, and how the contract of agency comes to an end. Agency is a vital business concept, as, in addition to the use of agents such as insurance brokers and estate agents and the like, agency is a fundamental concept in the law of partnership and company law.

Further reading

Ashton, C., et al., (2012) *Understanding Scots Law* 2nd edition. Edinburgh: W. Green. Chapter 10 pp.400-403.

Black, G., (ed), (2015) *Business Law in Scotland* 3rd edition. Edinburgh: W. Green. Chapter 9 pp. 349 - 367.

Combe, M., (2013) *Law Essentials: Commercial Law* Dundee: Dundee University Press. Chapter 3 pp. 37-46.

Davidson, F., and Macgregor, L., (2014) *Commercial Law in Scotland* 3rd edition. Edinburgh: W. Green. Chapter 2, pp. 67-84.

Macgregor, L., (2013) *The Law of Agency in Scotland.* Edinburgh: W. Green.

Macgregor, L., (2013) The agent's warranty of authority: thus far and no further. *Edinburgh Law Review* **17** (3): 398-409.

I Index

Table of Cases

Table of Malaysian Cases

Table of Statutes

Table of Scottish Statutes

Table of Statutory Instruments

Table of Scottish Statutory Instruments

Table of Malaysian Statutes

Printed in the United States
By Bookmasters